Men Without Work

MEN WITHOUT WORK

✄

America's Invisible Crisis

Nicholas Eberstadt

Templeton Press
300 Conshohocken State Road, Suite 500
West Conshohocken, PA 19428
www.templetonpress.org

Designed and typeset by Gopa & Ted2, Inc.

ISBN13: 978-1-59947-469-4

Library of Congress Cataloging-in-Publication Data on file.

Printed in the United States of America

17 18 19 20   10 9 8 7 6 5 4

For Christopher C. Demuth Sr.
Mentor, Colleague, Friend

≥≤

Contents

⋙⋘

Acknowledgments

❥❥

THIS BOOK, LIKE *A Nation of Takers* before it, was the idea of Susan Arellano, publisher of Templeton Press. Brilliant editor that she is, she somehow persuaded me that this effort too was actually my own idea. Susan is an utter delight as an intellectual compatriot. She is demanding in the best sense—encouraging her colleagues in the world of ideas to do their very best work, and even to try to exceed their own highest standards. Those on her Templeton Press team are professionals who epitomize grace under pressure. Their hard work is noted with truest authorial gratitude. Special thanks to Dave Reinhard for his deft and seamless reduction of my too-lengthy manuscript to a more reader-friendly length.

Although this is a slim volume, it required a considerable amount of data collection and quantitative analysis, including work with a variety of unpublished statistical files from the U.S. government and from nongovernment sources as well. I could never have produced this study without the splendid research assistance I enjoyed during this project.

Primus inter pares was Alexander Coblin, the extraordinarily talented scholar who was the main research assistant for this study. Alex's insights have enriched every chapter in this book. Alex also helped select an all-star team of interns whose work contributed significantly: Pat Hunley, Katherine Cole, Claire Chang Liu, and Gabe Anderson (whose "above-and-beyond" contributions during the completion of this study deserve a special salute). At a critical juncture in the study I was also aided in microdata analysis by Professor Joseph Price of Brigham Young University and an impressive squad of graduate students that he assembled for the task: Michael Gmeiner, Adam Shumway, Tanner Eastmond, and Jon McEwan. I owe a debt of gratitude to all these men and women. And it should go without saying that any errors in the following pages are mine alone.

My most important reader was my wife, Mary Eberstadt. This book, like the rest of my life, is the better for her insights.

Finally, the American Enterprise Institute (AEI) has been my professional home and intellectual haven for over thirty years. I owe the institution, and my friends and colleagues within it, more than can be expressed in any literary thumbnail. For reasons of space I thank here just two of many AEI friends and colleagues to whom I owe thanks: Arthur Brooks, AEI's current president; and Christopher DeMuth, his predecessor, AEI's president from 1986 through 2008.

On his tour of duty, Chris saved AEI and rededicated it. This book is dedicated to him.

Men Without Work

Introduction

❧

OVER THE PAST two generations, America has suffered a quiet catastrophe. That catastrophe is the collapse of work—for men. In the half century between 1965 and 2015, work rates for the American male spiraled relentlessly downward, and an ominous migration commenced: a "flight from work," in which ever-growing numbers of working-age men exited the labor force altogether. America is now home to an immense army of jobless men no longer even looking for work—more than seven million alone between the ages of twenty-five and fifty-five, the traditional prime of working life.

The collapse of work for America's men is arguably a crisis for our nation—but it is a largely invisible crisis. It is almost never discussed in the public square. Somehow, we as a nation have managed to ignore this problem for decades, even as it has steadily worsened. There is perhaps no other instance in the modern American experience of a social change of such consequence receiving so little consideration by concerned citizens, intellectuals, business leaders, and policymakers.

How big is the "men without work" problem today? Consider a single fact: in 2015, the work rate (or employment-to-population ratio) for American males ages twenty-five–to–fifty-four was slightly lower than it had been in 1940, which was at the tail end of the Great Depression.

The general decline of work for grown men and the dramatic, continuing expansion of a class of un-working males (including both those who are ostensibly able-bodied and in the prime of life) constitute a fundamentally new and unfamiliar reality for America. So very new and unfamiliar is this crisis, in fact, that it has until now very largely gone unnoticed and unremarked upon. Our news media, our pundits, and our major political parties have somehow managed to overlook this extraordinary dislocation almost altogether.

One reason the phenomenon has escaped notice is that there have been no obvious outward signs of national distress attending the American male's massive and continuing postwar exodus from paid employment: no national strikes, no great riots, no angry social paroxysms. In addition, America today is rich and, by all indications, getting even richer. Hence the end of work for a large, and steadily growing, share of working-age American men has been met to date with public complacency, in part because we evidently can afford to do so. And this is precisely the problem: for the genial indifference with which the rest of society has greeted the growing absence of adult men from the productive economy is in itself powerful testimony that *these men have become essentially dispensable.*

But the progressive detachment of so many adult American men from the reality and routines of regular paid labor poses a threat to our nation's future prosperity. It can only result in lower living standards, greater economic disparities, and slower economic growth than we might otherwise expect. And the troubles posed by this male flight from work are by no means solely economic. It is also a social crisis—and, I shall argue, a moral crisis. The growing incapability of grown men to function as breadwinners cannot help but undermine the American family. It casts those who nature designed to be strong into the role of dependents—on their wives or girl-friends, on their aging parents, or on government welfare. Among those who should be most capable of shouldering the burdens of civic responsibilities, it instead encourages sloth, idleness, and vices perhaps more insidious. Whether we choose to recognize it or not, this feature of the American condition—the new "men without work" normal—is inimical to the American tradition of self-reliance; it is subversive of our national ethos and arguably even of our civilization.

Our nation cannot begin to grapple with this challenge to our future unless we first understand its genesis, its dimensions, and its implications. In the following pages I attempt to offer a preliminary description of these.

PART I

❊

Men Without Work

CHAPTER 1

The Collapse of Work in the Second Gilded Age

⇒⇐

H OW IS THE U.S. economy doing these days? How are Americans themselves faring economically? These two closely related questions are central to any assessment of the well-being of our society and the health of our body politic. But these questions are more difficult to answer today than at any time in living memory.

This is not because our information-saturated era lacks facts and figures to take our nation's economic measure. Rather, it is because fundamental indicators of our country's economic outlook are far out of alignment with one another. Since the end of the twentieth century, the United States has witnessed an ominous and growing divergence among three trends that should ordinarily move together: wealth, output, and employment.

In terms of wealth creation, the twenty-first century appears to be off to a roaring start. It may look as if Americans have never had it so good and that the future is full of promise. Between early 2001 and late 2015, the net worth of

U.S. households and nonprofit institutions almost doubled, rising to $87 trillion (see figure 1.1).[1] In 2015, net worth averaged $270,000 per American—well over a million dollars per family of four. And this upsurge of wealth took place despite the terrible 2008 crash. In 2007, at the precrash apogee of estimated U.S. private wealth, total net worth of U.S. households and nonprofit institutions approached $68 trillion. Eight years later it was reportedly almost $20 trillion higher.

The U.S. economy also still looks like the world's unrivaled engine of wealth generation, notwithstanding the vaunted "rise of China." The Credit Suisse *Global Wealth Report*, for example, estimated that as of mid-year 2015, the United States possessed 34 percent of the entire world's personal ("household") wealth.[2] China ran a distant second at 9 percent. U.S. wealth holdings also exceeded those of Europe in spite of the fact that Europe's population is well over twice as large.

The value of U.S. real estate assets is at or near all-time highs today, and U.S. businesses and corporations appear to be thriving. In the summer of 2016, the Wilshire 5000 Full Cap Price Index set a new record, with a total calculated capitalization of over $22.5 trillion. Since stock prices are strongly shaped by expectations of future profits, it appears investors are counting on the happy days continuing for some time to come.

Impressive as this upswing in measured wealth appears on paper, though, there is also an element of artificiality to

FIGURE 1.1. UNITED STATES: HOUSEHOLDS AND NONPROFIT NET WORTH, QUARTERLY, 2000–2016 (TRILLIONS OF CURRENT U.S. DOLLARS)

Source: "Households and Nonprofit Organizations; Net Worth, Level," FRED Economic Data, last modified June 21, 2016, https://fred.stlouisfed.org/series/TNWBSHNO.

it. From the 2008 crash to this day, the Federal Reserve has deliberately inflated U.S. asset values through its unprecedented and prolonged "zero interest rate" policies, interventions that are, unsurprisingly, proving difficult to unwind.

A less cheerful picture emerges if we look at macroeconomic trends. Here, U.S. economic performance since the start of the century might best be described as mediocre and its future prospects no better than guarded.

The 2008 crash brought a severe recession—the worst since the Great Depression—and the recovery has been painfully slow and unusually weak. According to the Bureau of Economic Analysis, it took nearly four years for U.S. gross domestic product (GDP) to regain its late 2007 level. By contrast, in the sharp Reagan-era slump, the recovery took just twenty-one months. Our "Great Recession" was somewhat more akin to the Great Depression, when it took seven years to get back to 1929 levels. As of early 2016, the total value added for the U.S. economy was barely 10 percent higher than before the 2008 crash (see figure 1.2).

The situation is even more sobering with respect to real per capita output. It took the United States until mid-2014 to return to its late 2007 per capita production levels. As of the first quarter of 2016, U.S. per capita output was barely 3 percent higher than it had been eight years earlier. America, it seems, has suffered something close to a "lost decade." And the snapback in per capita GDP since its mid-2009 low has averaged only 1.1 percent a year, barely half of our long-run

FIGURE 1.2. UNITED STATES: REAL (2009 U.S. DOLLARS) GROSS DOMESTIC PRODUCT, QUARTERLY, 2000–2016 (EXPONENTIAL TREND LINE 1947–2007)

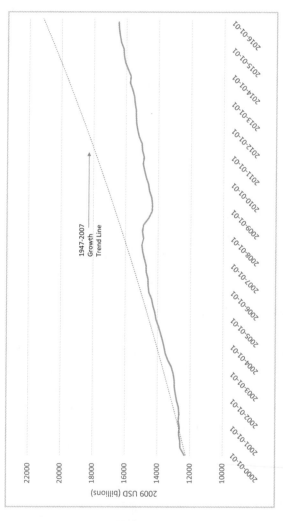

Source: "Real Gross Domestic Product," FRED Economic Data, last modified June 21, 2016, https://research.stlouisfed.org/fred2/series/GDPC1#.

annual per capita growth rate of 2.2 percent for 1947–2007 or 2.0 percent for 1987–2007. In other words, the U.S. economy currently is not nearly on track to return to its historic growth patterns.

Why is this recovery so much more fitful than other postwar recoveries?[3] Some economists suggest the reason has to do with the unusual nature of the Great Recession. Downturns born of major financial crises intrinsically require longer correction periods than business cycle downturns.[4] Others theorize that the scale of recent technological innovation is unrepeatable or that we have entered into an age of "secular stagnation" with low "natural real interest rates" consistent with significantly reduced investment demand.[5]

What is incontestable is that the ten-year moving average for U.S. per capita economic growth is lower today than at any time since the Korean War and that this slowdown commenced in the decade before the 2008 crash. As a result, a consensus among economists has developed in recent years redefining the growth potential of the U.S. economy downward. The U.S. Congressional Budget Office, for example, suggests that the "potential growth" rate for the U.S. economy at full employment of production factors has now dropped below 2 percent a year, implying a sustainable long-term annual per capita economic growth rate of 1 percent or less.[6]

The situation in the nation's labor force, for its part, is plainly awful (see fig 1.3). Between the start of the century and early 2016, the employment-to-population ratio ("work

FIGURE 1.3. EMPLOYMENT-TO-POPULATION RATIO FOR 20+ POPULATION: UNITED STATES, 2000–2016 (SEASONALLY ADJUSTED)

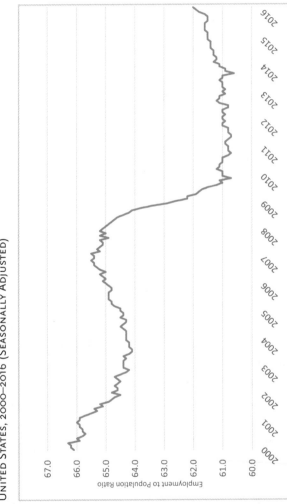

Source: "Labor Force Statistics from the Current Population Survey," LNS12300061, Bureau of Labor Statistics, retrieved on June 21, 2016, http://data.bls.gov/pdq/querytool.jsp?survey=ln.

rate") for Americans ages twenty and older declined by over four percentage points. Postwar America has never experienced anything like this. From peak to trough, the collapse in work rates for U.S. adults in the Bush–Obama years was roughly twice what had been the country's previous worst postwar recession in the 1980s. At that time, it took America five years to regain the adult work rates recorded at the start of 1980. This time, over a decade and a half into our new century, the U.S. job market has scarcely begun to claw its way back to the 2007 work rates. As can be seen in figure 1.3, U.S. adult work rates never recovered entirely after the 2001 recession.

The country's work rates virtually flatlined in the four years after the Great Recession (late 2009 to early 2014). So far as can be determined, this is the only "recovery" in U.S. history in which this basic labor market indicator almost completely failed to respond.

The work rate has improved since 2014, but it would be unwise to exaggerate that turnaround. As of early 2016, our adult work rate was still at its lowest level in three decades. *If our nation's work rate today were back to its start-of-the-century highs, approximately 10 million more Americans would currently have paying jobs.*[7]

Here, then, is the underlying contradiction of economic life in America's second Gilded Age: A period of what might at best be described as indifferent economic growth has somehow produced markedly more wealth for its wealth-holders and markedly less work for its workers.[8] This paradox may help explain a number of otherwise perplexing features of our time, such as the steep drop in popular satisfaction with the direction of the country, the increasing attraction of extremist voices in electoral politics, and why overwhelming majorities continue to tell public opinion pollsters, year after year, that our ever-richer America is still stuck in a recession.[9]

However bad our new employment profile may appear to the untutored eye, another facet looks even more dismal: employment trends for America's men. Male work rates have been in almost relentless decline, and not just since the dawn of the new century. Work rates for adult men have been falling for most of the post–World War II era. Between the early 1950s and today, the work rate for adult men has plummeted by more than eighteen percentage points. The drop since the Great Recession accounts for less than a quarter of the total long-term decline of twenty-plus employment-to-population ratios for U.S. men in the postwar era.

Many will find all this astounding. Others might object that I'm comparing apples and oranges here. After all, postwar America was an aging society, and older people tend to be out of the workforce. Would not a long-term fall in work rates exactly be expected in a prosperous and graying nation?

Alas, adjustments for changes in the postwar population structure do not come close to "correcting away" the collapse in male work rates. Even after appropriate corrections, work rates for U.S. men have still undergone a stunning decline. I shall detail the particulars of this sad saga in the following pages.

CHAPTER 2

Hiding in Plain Sight: An Army of Jobless Men, Lost in an Overlooked Depression

≽≼

MUCH CURRENT ANALYSIS of labor market conditions paints a cautiously optimistic—even unabashedly positive—picture of job trends. But easily accessible data demonstrate that we are, in reality, living through an extended period of extraordinary, Great Depression–scale underutilization of male manpower, and this severe "work deficit" for men has gradually worsened over time.

Expert opinions on U.S. labor market performance have been increasingly sanguine over the past year or so. A few select media headlines and quotations illustrate the emerging consensus:

- "The Jobless Numbers Aren't Just Good, They're Great" (August 2015, Bloomberg[1])
- "The Jobs Report Is Even Better Than It Looks" (November 2015, FiveThirtyEight[2])
- "Healthy Job Market at Odds with Global Gloom" (March 2016, *Wall Street Journal*[3])

- An excerpt from "Two Sides to Economic Recovery: Growth Stalls, While Jobs Soar" stated: "The job market, according to Labor Department figures released in recent months, is at its healthiest point since the boom of the late 1990s." (April 2016, *International New York Times*[4])
- "June's Super Jobs Report (July 2016, *Atlantic Monthly*[5])

In addition, U.S. economists and policymakers who have served under Republican and Democratic presidents maintain that today's U.S. economy is either near or at "full employment":

- "It is encouraging to see that the U.S. economy is approaching full employment with low inflation." (Ben Bernanke, former chairman of the Federal Reserve Board, October 2015[6])
- "The American economy is in good shape . . . we are essentially at full employment . . . tight labor markets are leading to increases in hourly earnings and in the producer prices of services." (Martin Feldstein, former chair of the President's Council of Economic Advisers and longtime director of the National Bureau of Economic Research, February 2016[7])
- "We are coming close to [the Federal Reserve's] assigned congressional goal of full employment. [Many measures of unemployment] really suggest a labor market that is vastly improved." (Janet Yellen, chairman of the Federal Reserve, April 2016[8])

All of these assessments draw upon data on labor market dynamics: job openings, new hires, "quit ratios," unemployment filings and the like. And all those data are informative—as far as they go. But they miss also something, a big something: the deterioration of work rates for American men.

The pronouncements above stand in stark contrast to the trends illustrated in figure 2.1, which track officially estimated work rates for U.S. men over the postwar era (see figure 2.1).

The federal government did not begin releasing continuous monthly data on U.S. employment until after World War II. By any broad measure, U.S. employment-to-population rates for civilian, noninstitutionalized men in 2015 were close to their lowest levels on record—and vastly lower than levels in earlier postwar decades.[9]

Between 1948 and 2015, the work rate for U.S. men twenty and older fell from 85.8 percent to 68.2 percent. Thus the proportion of American men twenty and older without paid work more than doubled, from 14 percent to almost 32 percent. Granted, the work rate for adult men in 2015 was over a percentage point higher than 2010 (its all-time low). But purportedly "near full employment" conditions notwithstanding, the work rate for the twenty-plus male was more than a fifth lower in 2015 than in 1948.

Of course, the twenty-plus work rate measure includes men sixty-five and older, men of classic retirement age. But when the sixty-five-plus population is excluded, work rates

Figure 2.1. Employment-to-Population Ratio, U.S. Males, Selected Age Groups, 1948–2016 (Seasonally Adjusted)

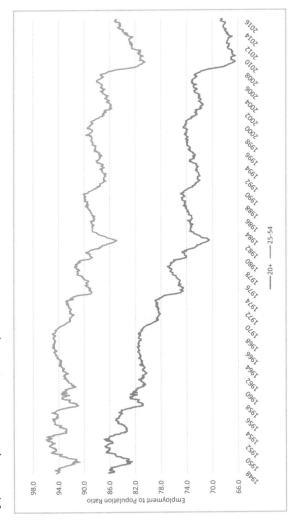

Source: "Labor Force Statistics from the Current Population Survey," LNS12300025, LNS12300061, Bureau of Labor Statistics, retrieved on May 16, 2016, http://data.bls.gov/pdq/querytool.jsp?survey=ln.

trace a long march downward here, too. By 2015, nearly 22 percent of U.S. men between the ages of twenty and sixty-five were not engaged in paid work of any kind, and the work rate for this grouping was nearly 12.5 percentage points below its 1948 level. In short, the fraction of U.S. men from ages twenty–to–sixty-four not at work in 2015 was 2.3 times higher than it had been in 1948.

As for "prime-age" men—the twenty-five–to–fifty-four group that historically always has the highest employment—work rates fell from 94.1 percent in 1948 to 84.3 percent in 2015. Under today's "near-full employment" norm, a monthly average of nearly one in six prime-age men had no paying job of any kind.

Though the work rate for prime-age men has recovered to some degree since 2010, the latest report as of this writing (July 2016) is barely on par with the lowest-ever Bureau of Labor Statistics (BLS) reading before the Crash of 2008 (the depths of the early 1980s recession). In 2015, the proportion of prime-age men without jobs was over 2.5 times higher than in 1948. Indeed, 1948 work rates for men in their late fifties and early sixties were slightly higher than for prime-age men today.

Even more shocking is the comparison of work rates for prime-age men today with those from the prewar Depression era.

During the Depression era, we did not possess our current official statistical apparatus for continuously monitoring employment conditions. Our postwar statistical apparatus for continuously monitoring employment conditions only came in response to the prewar employment crisis. Consequently, our main source of information on Depression-era employment comes from our decennial population censuses. As fate would have it, the Great Depression spanned two national censuses, the 1930 census, near the start of the Depression, and the 1940 census, near its end.[10] We contra-

Table 2.1. U.S. Male Employment-to-Population Ratios: Today vs. Selected Depression Years

YEAR AND SOURCE	EMPLOYMENT TO POPULATION RATIO, MEN 20–64 (PERCENTAGE OF CIVILIAN NON-INSTITUTIONAL POPULATION)	EMPLOYMENT TO POPULATION RATIO, MEN 25–54 (PERCENTAGE OF CIVILIAN NONINSTITUTIONAL POPULATION)
2015 (BLS)	78.4	84.4
1940 (Census)	81.3	86.4
1930 (Census)	88.2*	91.2**

Source: For 2015: Bureau of Labor Statistics, Labor Force Statistics from the Current Population Survey, LNS12300025, LNS12300061, http://data.bls.gov/pdq/querytool.jsp?survey=ln. Accessed May 16, 2016. For 1940: Derived from http://www.jstor.org/stable/117246?seq=1_page_scan_tab_contents; http://censusacn.adobeaemcloud.com'library/publications/1943/dec/population-labor-forcesample.html_Table_1; http://www2.census.gov/library/publications/decennial/1940/population-institutional--population/08520028ch2.pdf; http://www/dtic.mil/dtic/tr/fulltext/u2/a954007.pdf. Accessed August 5, 2016. For 1930: http://digital.library.unt.edu/ark:/67531/metadc26169/m1/1/high_res_d/R40655_2009Jun19. pdf. Accessed March 2, 2016.
Notes: *Calculated for total numerated population, not civilian noninstitutional population; **Twenty-five–to–forty-four male population corresponding male twenty-five–to–forty-four ratio for 2015 would be 85.3 percent.

pose male employment patterns then and now in table 2.1.

According the 1940 census, the work rate for civilian non-institutional men twenty–to–sixty-four years old was 81.3 percent. In 2015, that rate was 78.4 percent. The work rate for prime-age males in 1940 was reported to be 86.5 percent, two points higher than in 2015 and about a point and a half higher than readings thus far for 2016. In other words, work rates for men appear to be lower today than they were late in the Great Depression when the civilian unemployment rate ran above 14 percent.[11] Furthermore, the work rate for American men is manifestly lower today than it was in 1930, to judge by returns from the 1930 census.

Admittedly, the comparison is not straightforward, since the 1930 census used different questions about employment status than we use today and did not break out "civilian noninstitutional population" from the total adult population. Nonetheless, the Census Bureau has harmonized those 1930 employment figures with modern definitions of work and joblessness.[12] By these reconstructions, the 1930 ratio for employment to total population for men twenty–to–sixty-four was over 88 percent. Among men twenty-five to forty-four (prime work ages for that era) the ratio for employment to total population was over 91 percent. In 2015, the official work rate for working-age men twenty–to–sixty-four was nearly ten percentage points below this 1930 figure (78.4 percent vs. 88.2 percent) and for men twenty-five to forty-four, the nominal gap was nearly six points (85.3 percent vs.

91.2 percent). These numerical differences, I should note, *understate* slightly the true work rate gap between adult men in 1930 and today, since the 1930 numbers do not exclude men in the armed forces, prisons, long-term hospitalization, etc., from the demographic denominator by which current work rates for the "civilian noninstitutional" population are calculated.

To be clear, the employment disaster in the depths of the Great Depression was unquestionably worse than it was in either 1930 or 1940.[13] For better or worse, however, we only have these two census data points for that era's labor market conditions, and current data indicate that work rates for American men are *lower* today than in either of these years. It is thus meaningful to talk about work rates for American men today as being at Depression-era levels. In fact, they are more depressed than those recorded in particular years of the Great Depression.

Just how great is our current "work deficit" for American men? One reasonable benchmark for measuring that gap might be the mid-1960s. Then, the U.S. economy was strong and labor markets functioned at genuinely full employment levels.

Between 1965 and 2015, work rates for men twenty and older fell by over 13 percent. Population aging cannot account for most of this massive decline: nearly four-fifths of that drop was due to age-specific declines in work rates or 1967–2015 (the period for which more detailed data are

FIGURE 2.2. AGE-STRUCTURE ADJUSTED EMPLOYMENT-TO-POPULATION RATIO,
U.S. MALES 20–64, ANNUAL 1967–2015

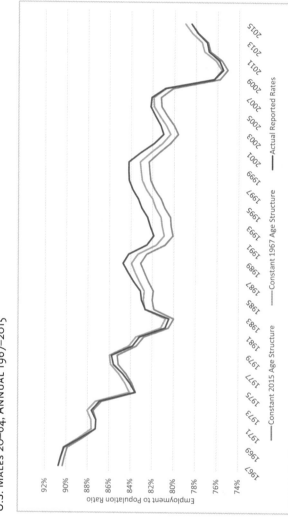

Source: "Labor Force Statistics from the Current Population Survey," 20+ LNS12300025, 64+ LNU02300199, Bureau of Labor Statistics, retrieved on May 17, 2016, http://data.bls.gov/pdq/querytool.jsp?survey=ln.

available for such calculations). Over these same years, work rates for men in the broad twenty–to–sixty-four group fell from 90 percent to less than 79 percent. In other words, over the two generations, the fraction of men without jobs of any sort in the broad twenty–to–sixty-four group went from 10 percent of the total to almost 22 percent). Almost none of that decline can be attributed to changes in age structure (see figure 2.2). For the critical prime-age group (men twenty-five–to–fifty-four), work rates dropped over this half century from about 94 percent to just over 84 percent. Consequently, the percentage of wholly jobless prime-age men shot from 6 percent to nearly 16 percent.

If we look at the long-term trends over the postwar era, we see an eerie and radical transformation in the condition of prime-age men: the unrelenting ratcheting upward in the fraction of men without any paid employment (see figure 2.3). In the decade of the 1960s, monthly averages indicated that one in sixteen prime-age American men were not at work. By the 1990s, the ratio had jumped to one in eight. In the current decade (January 2010 to June 2016), the ratio has dropped below one in six for an average of 17.5 percent of prime-age men with no paid work in the past month.[14]

What does all this mean for the current "work deficit" for grown men? If age-specific work rates for the civilian noninstitutional adult population had simply held constant from 1965 to today, over 10.5 million additional men ages twenty–to–sixty-four would have been working for pay in

FIGURE 2.3. PERCENTAGE OF CIVILIAN NONINSTITUTIONAL PRIME-AGE (25–54) MALE POPULATION WITHOUT PAID EMPLOYMENT: UNITED STATES 1948–2016 (SEASONALLY ADJUSTED)

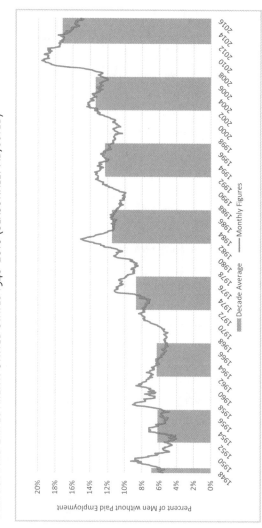

Source: Bureau of Labor Statistics, "Labor Force Statistics from the Current Population Survey," Employed LNS12000061, Civilian Noninstitutional Population LNU00000061; Bureau of Labor Statistics, retrieved on June 21, 2016, www.bls.gov/data.

2015 America, including an additional 6 million men in the prime twenty-five–to–fifty-four group.[15]

In one important respect, however, this 10.5-million-plus figure overstates today's "deficit" for men. The reason: it fails to account for the steady increase in education and training for adult men over the past five decades. Education and work-related training can temporarily take work-minded men out of the workforce. It's critical to make adjustments for these factors to get a meaningful sense of the true falloff in paid employment for men in modern America.

Unfortunately, making these adjustments is not such a straightforward task. Statistics on training are notoriously limited, inconsistent, and contradictory.[15] Numbers on formal education can also be problematic. Nevertheless, by 2014 (the latest figures available), nearly a million more men in their early twenties were in school than would have been the case with 1965 enrollment ratios.[16] For men twenty-five–to–sixty-four, the corresponding number exceeded 1.6 million.[17] These numbers suggest that at least 2.5 million more adult men were in education or training in 2014 than in 1965.

Of course, not all of these men would have been out of work pursuing work-related education or training. It's actually quite the contrary. The overwhelming majority of adult male job trainees appear to be job holders already. That is the nature of job-related training. As for formal education, most men of all adult ages enrolled in formal schooling are also in the workforce. They are typically part-time student workers or part-time working students. In 2014, according to Current Population Survey (CPS) data from the Census Bureau, 55 percent of all men twenty and older enrolled in schooling were simultaneously working paid jobs. The same was true for nearly 70 percent of men twenty-five–to–fifty-four years of age.[18] So the real question becomes what proportion of the additional men in school or training were out of the workforce because they were in school or training.

Roughly speaking, CPS data indicate that adult schooling *per se* is currently taking about a million more working-age men out of the paid workforce today than would have been the case if the twenty-plus population conformed to 1965-era enrollment ratios.[19] (Not all of this schooling is directly or even indirectly employment related.) If we deduct this million from the 10.5 million figure above, the "corrected" total for 2015 would be approximately 9.5 million.

In sum, even after (generously) adjusting for today's demanding regimen of adult schooling and training, the net "jobs deficit" in 2015 for men twenty–to–sixty-four in relation to 1965-era work patterns would come out to a number approaching 10 million. The implied employment deficit works out to around 1.2 million for men in their early twenties and about 5.5 million for prime-age men twenty-five–to–fifty-four, with the remainder being men in their late fifties and early sixties.

If 1965-style employment patterns applied today, an additional 10-plus percent of America's civilian noninstitutional male population between the ages of twenty and sixty-five would have been working and earning a paycheck in 2015, even after taking educational expansion into account. We would also have about 10 percent more men at work in the prime-age years than we do today.

Romans used the word "decimation" to describe the loss of a tenth of a given unit of men. The United States has suffered something akin to a decimation of its male workforce over the past fifty years. This disturbing situation is our "new normal." No less disturbing is the fact that the general public and political elites have uncritically accepted this American decimation as today's "new normal."

Today's received wisdom holds that the United States is now at or near "full employment." An alternative view would hold that, by not-so-distant historic standards, the nation today is short of full employment by nearly 10 million male workers (to say nothing of the additional current "jobs deficit" for women). Unlike the dead soldiers in Roman antiquity, our decimated men still live and walk among us, though in an existence without productive economic purpose. We might say those many millions of men without work constitute a sort of invisible army, ghost soldiers lost in an overlooked, modern-day depression.

CHAPTER 3

Postwar America's Great Male Flight from Work

≥≤

THE DRAMATIC DROP in employment for American men over two generations—nearly 10 million fewer jobs for men twenty–to–sixty-four years of age in 2015 than would have been expected at 1965 work rates, even after adjusting for population aging and educational expansion—presents us with a sort of "dog not barking" riddle. The quiet postwar collapse of male work did not occasion great political eruption, breakdowns, or convulsions. Nor has the de facto disappearance of some 10 million able-bodied men from the paid workforce sparked an acute shortage of workers for the U.S. economy. (True, American business interests complain today of the lack of skilled labor with particular qualifications for specific specialized occupations, but this is a cry that has been sounded for decades.) How do so many millions of "missing men" disappear from U.S. payrolls today with so little attendant sociopolitical upheaval? Why has this decimation not commanded attention as a national emergency?

Two big postwar changes in the U.S. labor market help answer this riddle.

The first is the historic postwar transformation in the nature of women's work. This epic change was not, of course, peculiar to America. It unfolded in all Westernized industrial democracies, and elsewhere as well. Before World War II, the exclusive economic activity for the overwhelming majority of U.S. women was unpaid labor at home. Today the overwhelming majority of women—including women with young children—engage in at least some remunerated employment outside the family. Needless to say, this shift has opened up new prospects for prosperity, as well as new horizons of economic independence and autonomy.[1]

The tremendous expansion of economic opportunities for U.S. women created a massive new supply of workers in the postwar economy. The share of women with paid work skyrocketed in every age group and doubled for women between twenty-five and sixty-four. For women twenty-five–to–fifty-four, the work rate was 34 percent in 1948; in 2015, it topped 70 percent. In arithmetic terms, this enormous influx of new workers completely offset the decline in work rates for prime-age men—and then some (see figure 3.1). Thanks to the progressive entry of ever-greater proportions of women into the workforce, overall work rates for every grouping of Americans between the ages of twenty and sixty-four also increased substantially between the late 1940s and the late 1990s. Around the late 1990s, however, the escalation of work rates for U.S. women stalled and, over the past decade and a half, fell from their all-time highs. Only then did the overall work rate for U.S. adults begin to register a decline.

FIGURE 3.1. EMPLOYMENT-TO-POPULATION RATIOS FOR 25–54 POPULATION BY SEX AND BOTH SEXES COMBINED: UNITED STATES, 1948–2016 (SEASONALLY ADJUSTED)

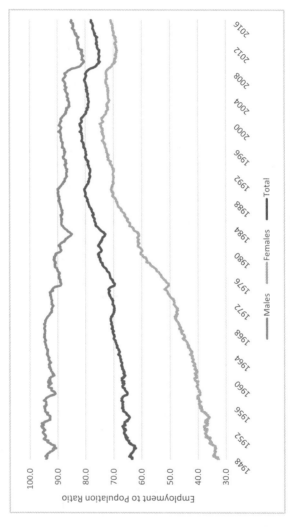

Source: "Labor Force Statistics from the Current Population Survey," LNU02300026, LNU02300062, LNU00000026, LNU02000026, LNU02000354. Bureau of Labor Statistics, retrieved on June 21, 2016, http://data.bls.gov/pdq/querytool.jsp?survey=ln.

For two full generations, the upsurge of employment for women disguised the steady decline in work for men. It also changed the complexion of the population not at work. The prime-age population without paid employment become ever-more "male" in the decades since 1948—mainly through a huge rise in the number of prime-age men without jobs (see figure 3.2). In 1948, men made up a little more than a tenth of working-age (twenty–to–sixty-four) Americans without jobs. By 2015, however, they made up nearly two-fifths of this population.

The second overarching change came in the nature of male participation in the labor market—or rather, the declining likelihood of such participation. Postwar America has witnessed a long-term and continuing exodus of working-age men from the workforce. Ever-greater numbers of working-age men simply have dropped out—some for a while and some forever—from the competition for jobs. These men have established a new and alternative lifestyle to the age-old male quest for a paying job. Members of this caste can, at least, expect to scrape by in an employment-free existence, and membership in the caste is, in an important sense, voluntary. Not only are those in this caste not actively looking for work, but only a small minority report that they've left the labor force because they cannot find a job (the classic definition of a "discouraged worker"[2]).

The growing absence of these men from the productive economy has not provoked social disorder or other unpleasant

Figure 3.2. Nonworking* U.S. Population, Ages 20–64: Female vs. Male, 1948–Present, in Millions (Seasonally Unadjusted)

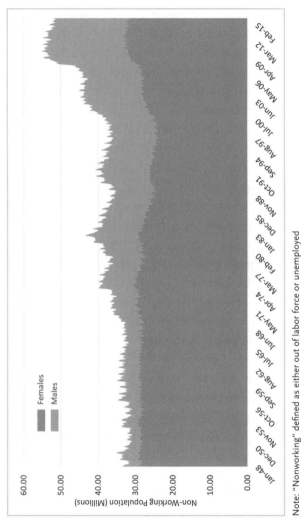

Note: "Nonworking" defined as either out of labor force or unemployed

Source: "Labor Force Statistics from the Current Population Survey," Men 20+ LNS12300025; Men 65+ LNU02300199; Women 20+ LNS15000026, Women 65+ LNU05000354, retrieved on February 12, 2016, Bureau of Labor Statistics, www.bls.gov/data.

"security and control" issues, precisely because this flight from work has ostensibly been a willing outmigration. This mass retreat from the workforce has been possible to ignore because these men are largely socially invisible and inert, written off or discounted by society and, perhaps, all too often, even by themselves.

Until roughly the outbreak of World War II, the overwhelming majority of nonfarm working-age American men fell into one of two employment categories: working a paid job or unemployed. There was no "third way" for healthy, able-bodied males. Life then was much closer to the bone than today. There were few social guarantees of any sort. The prospect of being without regular employment filled most men with dread. To be jobless was to court financial disaster, and the specter of long-term joblessness was terrifying to anyone responsible for supporting a family.

In today's America, by contrast, the taxonomy of employment is no longer so black-and-white. There are now not two but three possible work categories for civilian, noninstitutionalized working-age men: (1) employed, (2) unemployed but seeking work, and (3) neither working nor seeking work (i.e., living outside the labor force altogether).

This "third way" was previously unthinkable as a voluntary option (at least for the self-respecting, and for those without independent wealth). Today's no-work life is hardly a pathway to economic success, as we shall see. On the other hand, neither does it consign the growing numbers of no-work men to a life sentence of destitution and ruin. The United States today is evidently rich enough to carry, after a fashion, a growing contingent of working-age men who subsist without either engaging in or seeking paid employment. In short, a life without work (or the search for work) has become a viable option for today's prime-age male—and ever-greater numbers of them seem to be choosing this option.

The spread and general social toleration of the workless lifestyle for men, of course, could not have taken place without a normative sea change as well. An earlier era had terms for sturdy men who chose to sit on the economic sidelines, living off the toil or bounty of others. None were kind or forgiving. I shall touch upon aspects of this great change in norms and mores later.

The rise of the un-working American man underscores the antiquated and misleading nature of our major official measure of labor market health: the so-called unemployment rate. By that familiar yardstick, the employment situation for prime-age men in 2015 and early 2016 looks pretty good. Joblessness for prime-age men in early 2016 was a little over 4 percent. It was lower than for most years over the past half century and about the same level as in the economic upswings of the late Kennedy or the mid-Clinton presidencies. Indeed, it was lower than at any point during the long Reagan expansion. Further, by the metric of prime-age male unemployment, the pace of recovery from the "Great Recession" looks to have been more rapid and dynamic than many recessions in the postwar era.

But the unemployment rate was created in an age when mass withdrawal of working-age men from the workforce was inconceivable. Consequently, it takes no account of the very group that has been growing most rapidly within America's postwar male working-age population: a group that now vastly outnumbers those formally unemployed.

Yes, the unemployment rate still has its uses. Administrators, for example, still need to know how many unemployment insurance checks to mail out each month. But it no longer serves as a reliable predictor for the numbers or proportions of persons who are not working—or, for that matter, for those who *are* working. The relationship between the work rate and the unemployment rate for prime-age men has eroded over in the postwar era, and this erosion markedly accelerated after 1965.

We can better understand how the unemployment rate became an outdated and increasingly flawed metric if we trace the flight from work by men over the postwar period. We can start by looking at this phenomenon within the prime-age cohort.

Between 1948 and 1965, the absolute number of prime-age men outside the workforce rose only very slightly, from 935,000 to just under 1.1 million.[3] Between 1965 and 2015, however, these totals exploded. By 2015, the number of prime-age inactive men was over 7 million—6.5 times higher than it had been half a century earlier. In this fifty-year period, America's population of un-working prime-age men grew by almost 3.8 percent per annum. By contrast, the total male population twenty-five–to–fifty-four years of age roughly doubled in size, growing on average by 1.3 percent annually over these decades. The slowest growing component of the prime-age male population was men working or seeking work. This component expanded by just 75 percent, or by 1.1 percent a year.

For fifty years, in other words, the numbers of prime-age men neither working nor looking for work has grown more than three times faster—nearly four times faster—than the number who are working or looking for work. This same general trend holds for broader groupings of working-age men. For men twenty–to–sixty-four, for example, the numbers not in the labor force more than quintupled between 1965 and 2015, soaring from 3 million to 16 million. While the overall male twenty–to–sixty-four labor force grew by about 1 percent a year over these decades, the ranks of their economically inactive counterparts were swelling more than three times that fast.

The labor force participation rate (LFPR)—job holders and job seekers relative to the population from which they are drawn—for prime-age men fell from a monthly average of 96.6 percent in 1965 to just 88.2 percent in 2015. Expressed another way, the proportion of economically inactive men of prime working age leapt from 3.4 percent in 1965 to 11.8

percent in 2015. And for men twenty–to–sixty-four years of age, LFPRs fell from 92.9 percent to 78.8 percent—meaning the economically inactive share of prime-age males tripled, rocketing up from 7 percent to 21 percent. For all men twenty and older, LFPRs fell from to 83.6 to 71.5 percent. With either 1967 or 2015 constant population structures, the decline would have been on the order of nine percentage points between 1967 and 2015, meaning that close to three-fourths of this decline was *not* due to aging effects.

Thanks to this steady, ongoing exodus from the labor force, the economically inactive have come to eclipse the unemployed as the main category of men without jobs in modern America (see figure 3.3). From 1948 through 1965, there was a rough balance between the numbers of prime-age men who were out of work but looking for a job and those out of the labor force altogether, neither working nor seeking work. In fact, the unemployed slightly outnumbered the un-working. Between January 1948 and December 1965, an average of eighty-seven prime-age men were not in the labor force for every one hundred unemployed. Between 1965 and 2015, that balance radically shifted. By 2015, there were on average three un-working prime-age men for each prime-age man out of work but looking for a job in any given month. At no point in the past two decades—not a single month—have the unemployed exceeded the economically inactive among America's prime-age men. Even in the depths of the Great Recession (February 2010), more men

FIGURE 3.3. MALE 25–54 UNEMPLOYED VS. NOT IN LABOR FORCE (NILF): UNITED STATES, JANUARY 1948–MAY 2016 (SEASONALLY UNADJUSTED)

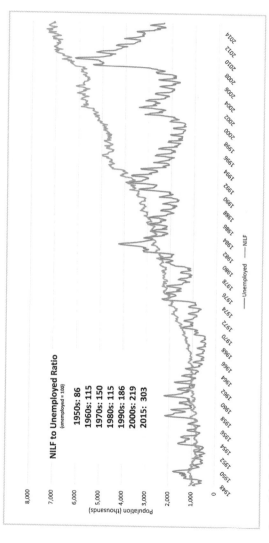

NILF to Unemployed Ratio
(unemployed = 100)

1950s:	86
1960s:	115
1970s:	150
1980s:	115
1990s:	186
2000s:	219
2015:	303

—— Unemployed —— NILF

Source: "Labor Force Statistics from the Current Population Survey," LNS13000061, LNU05000061, Bureau of Labor Statistics, retrieved on June 19, 2015; www.bls.gov/data.

were completely inactive economically than unemployed and looking for work.[4]

As already noted, many men not working or seeking work today are attempting to improve their employability through adult schooling and training. But work-related education is hardly the main driver of the ongoing male flight from work. In 2014 (latest data available) the number of prime-age men enrolled in some schooling, but not in the workforce, numbered just under eight hundred thousand. In that same year, the monthly average of prime-age males not in the labor force was 7.2 million. Such adult part- or full-time students accounted for less than one in nine economically inactive men of prime-age. Over 6.4 million prime-age men were neither engaged in the workforce nor in education in 2014—more than a tenth of the entire civilian noninstitutional cohort.

As of 2014, America thus had two and a half prime-age men who were both un-working and not in school for each one who was jobless but seeking work. It is difficult to make the precise comparison with 1965, owing to the surprising difficulty of obtaining employment data for that year for adults who were both enrolled in school and working at least part time.[5] In 1965 there were roughly 1.1 million civilian noninstitutional prime-age men outside the labor force but over seven hundred thousand men in that same age group reportedly enrolled in schooling. If we assume the same work rates for prime-age male students applied then as they apply today—a nontrivial "if"—the average monthly total for prime-age economically idle men (known in Britain as "neither employed nor in education or training" [NEET]) would have amounted to fewer than nine hundred thousand in 1965. Set that nine hundred thousand yearly total against a monthly average of the more than eight hundred thousand jobless who were seeking paid employment. Thus, America's ratio of prime-age NEET males to prime-age unemployed males may have tilted from rough parity in 1965 to something more on the order of 2.5:1 in a half century.

Accordingly, more than eight times as many prime-age men were economically inactive and not pursuing education in 2014 than in 1965. Over those same years, the share of such more or less wholly economically idle prime-age men would have nearly quadrupled to over a tenth of the entire cohort.

For the broader twenty–to–sixty-four grouping, the trends would be similar. By our rough estimates and assumptions, in 1965 one man out of twenty-two in the corresponding civilian noninstitutional population was economically inactive and also not in school. For 2014, the figure was more than one man in seven. The men of conventional working age who had made a full or near-full retreat from the workforce would have been six and a half times greater in 2014 than in 1965. This NEET group grew nearly three times faster than the civilian working-age male population and well over three times faster than the male working-age labor force.[6]

One final aspect of the U.S. postwar male flight from

work merits mention here: its relentless intergenerational momentum. It is not just that LFPRs have deteriorated for certain age groups or specific periods. Rather, the process has progressively depressed every successive rising cohort's LFPRs over the course of the prime working ages (see figure 3.4). (This chart comes from a 2016 study on declining prime-age male LFPRs by the president's Council of Economic Advisors [CEA], one of the few research groups in America today to devote such attention to that problem.)

Figure 3.4 traces U.S. LFPRs over the course of the prime-age working years for men born each successive decade from the 1930s onward. On average, a man seems less likely to be in the labor force than his older brother, who in turn is less likely to be in the workforce than his father, or his father's older brother.

This chart highlights a seemingly inexorable male detachment from the workforce and work—a detachment that is transforming our society, our economy, and American men themselves. It is a detachment that has proceeded apace in good times and bad.

FIGURE 3.4. Prime-Age Male Labor Force Participation over the Life Cycle by Birth Cohort

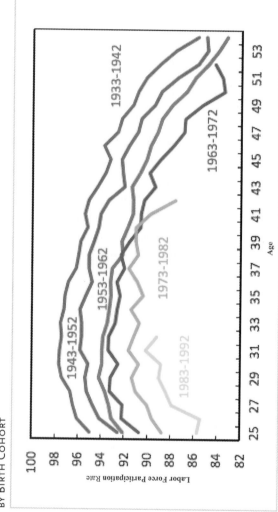

Source: "The Long-Term Decline in Prime-Age Male Labor Force Participation," Council of Economic Advisers, retrieved on July 27, 2016. Original source is Current Population Survey (Annual Social and Economic Supplement), CEA Calculations, Bureau of Labor Statistics.

CHAPTER 4

America's Great Male Flight from Work in Historical and International Perspective

≥≤

THAT AMERICAN MEN today should toil less than their fathers or their fathers' fathers is in itself no surprise. This is a predictable consequence of mass prosperity. Free-time is a luxury. Affluent societies produce more of this luxury than poorer societies, and affluent peoples avail themselves of this luxury more than their less-affluent forebears. This is common across people, places, and time.

The postwar flight from work by American men, however, does not neatly fit into this general tableau. There is no obvious reason to expect that the widely desired rise in free-time should necessarily mean that a growing share of working-age adults engaged in no paid work have *nothing but* free-time—much less that prime-age men should be in the vanguard of this new leisure class of un-workers.

On the contrary, America's postwar male flight from work is historically and internationally peculiar, if not anomalous. Our declining LFPRs among males are certainly not "typical" of other modern Westernized societies. Although Americans who actually work spend markedly longer hours at the job than their counterparts in affluent European countries and in Japan, the share of prime-age American men who do no work at all is also much higher than among our affluent international peers.

Roughly three generations of quantitative economic research have provided us with an increasingly comprehensive picture of how modern economic growth (what some term "structural transformation") changes both productive capacities and standards of living. As Nobel Economics Laureate Robert William Fogel has observed,

> Over the course of the twentieth century, annual hours of work [in Western Europe and America] have fallen by nearly half, so much so that the household head in a rich country now usually works only about seventeen hundred hours per year in the marketplace. Indeed, on the average day, he spends more hours at leisure than at work.[1]

As for the United States, Dora Costa, an economist at the University of California Los Angeles, concluded in 1998,

> The length of the work day fell sharply between the 1880s when the typical worker labored ten hours a day six days a week and 1920 when his counterpart worked an eight hour day six-days a week. By

1940 the typical work schedule was eight hours a day five days a week. Although further reductions in work time largely took the form of increases in vacations, holidays, sick days, personal leave, and earlier retirement, time diary studies suggest that the work day has continued to trend downwards to less than eight hours a day.[2]

With rising incomes and attendant gains in personal wealth, older American men were no longer consigned to laboring until death. The convention of "retirement" arose well before the New Deal or Social Security. By 1930, Costa noted, over 40 percent of American men sixty-five and older were no longer working or looking for work—nearly twice the fraction in 1880.[3] With prosperity rising, a small but growing fraction of men in their early sixties and late fifties also began to retire early.

Nevertheless, the overwhelming majority of American men fifty-five–to–sixty-four were still part of the labor force in the early postwar era. In 1950, according to the Bureau of Labor Statistics, LFPRs for this group were 87 percent, and there was no analogous case for retirement on the part of men who were in the prime of working life (ages twenty-five–to–fifty-four). In fact, what may be most striking about work trends for prime-age American men in the early postwar era is that their LFPRs actually rose. The increase was not immense, of course, since LFPRs right after the war were already well above 95 percent. In retrospect, what's remarkable is that they rose at all. In the late 1940s, LFPRs for prime-age men averaged 96.6 percent; for the decade of the fifties, 97.1 percent. LFPRs did not fall back below their 1948 levels until the late 1960s.

There is no mystery to this improvement in early postwar LFPRs. Prime-age American men were becoming healthier, better educated, and more capable of entering the labor market.[4] Between 1948 and 1960, as the proportion of prime-age civilian men not in the labor force shrank from 3.4 percent to 3.0 percent, the risk of death during prime work years for an American man likewise fell from nearly 17 percent to less than 15 percent. (By 2014, that risk had fallen to barely 8 percent.)[5] Educational attainment was likewise on the upswing. Between 1947 and 1959, the fraction of U.S. men twenty-five and older with a high school degree jumped from 23 percent to 42 percent. (By 2015, it was 88 percent.) For men in their late twenties, it went from 49 percent to 64 percent. (By 2015, it was 91 percent.)[6] The wonder here is that workforce participation over the past half century deteriorated despite these positive trends.

This prime-age male flight from work is a wonder all the more when set against other "traditional" members of the Organisation for Economic Co-operation and Development (OECD; see figure 4.1). This de facto club of affluent, aid-giving Western democracies includes Japan, Canada, Australia, New Zealand, and eighteen Western European nations

FIGURE 4.1. Labor Force Participation Rates for Men Ages 25–54: United States vs. 22 "Original" Organisation for Economic Co-operation and Development (OECD) Member States, 1960–2015

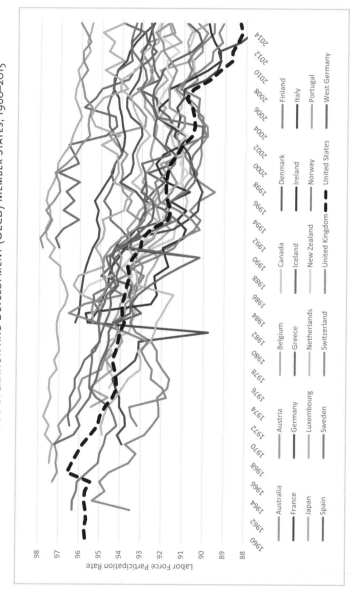

Source: "Labour Force Participation Rate," OECD Data, retrieved on June 21, 2015, https://data.oecd.org/emp/labour-force-participation-rate.htm.

as well as the United States. Today, the United States ranks twenty-second among these twenty-three countries in prime-age male labor force participation, underperformed only by Italy. This was not always so. In 1966, the United States was in the middle among countries for which such data were available. In all of these countries, LFPRs for prime-age men declined at least a bit over the next five decades. In none—not even Italy—did LFPRs fall as far and as fast as in the United States.

U.S. LFPRs, moreover, look distinctly poorer for prime-age males than for other male age groups. For the overall male fifteen–to–sixty-four grouping, the United States ranked fifteenth in 2014, subpar but not bottom of the barrel. For the fifty-five–to–sixty-four group, U.S. men ranked tenth and fifth for seniors sixty-five and older. So not only does America's flight from work by prime-age men appear extraordinary compared to our economic peers: it appears even greater when compared to U.S. and international labor force partic-ipation patterns for other adults overall.[7]

In no sense can the U.S. flight from work by prime-age males be deemed "normal" or "routine" for countries at our "general stage of socioeconomic development." Rather, something in today's America seems especially amiss.

Contrast LFPRs for prime-age men in the United States with those in some of Europe's most sclerotic labor mar-kets: France and the debt-stressed European Union nations of Portugal, Italy, Ireland, Greece, and Spain (the PIIGS),

Figure 4.2. Portugal, Italy, Ireland, Greece, and Spain (PIIGS) plus France vs. U.S. Labor Force Participation Rates: Men Ages 25–54, 1960–2015

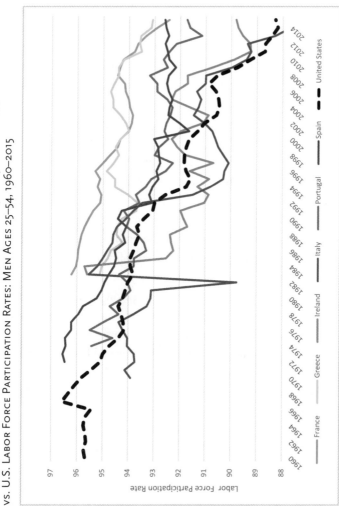

Source: "Labour Force Participation Rate," OECD Data, retrieved on June 21, 2015, https://data.oecd.org/emp/labour-force-participation-rate.htm.

which suffered (and, in some cases, still suffer) severe adjustment troubles as a result of the 2008 crash (see figure 4.2). American trends in prime-age male LFPRs are actually less favorable than in France, much less the PIIGS economies. The flight from work has been markedly more pronounced in the United States since at least the 1970s, the period for which data for all countries are commonly available. Both Greece and France currently report prime-age male LFPRs roughly five percentage points higher than United States—higher levels than the United States has seen since the mid-1980s. Greece's well-publicized fiscal debt and economic crises in 2014 nearly led to its expulsion from the European Union. Yet a far higher proportion of prime-age men were out of the U.S. workforce that year—almost four-fifths again as many.

And so the puzzle: America has a more robust economy, a more flexible and dynamic labor market, and a more limited welfare state than any of these six countries. But it has failed to keep its younger men in the workforce at the level that these struggling nations (with the arguable exception of Italy) have achieved. Why?

Japan presents a different sort of contrast. The labor market is less distorted there than in France and the PIIGS countries, and the Japanese welfare state is, generally speaking, less hypertrophied.[8] Still, Japan has famously suffered a generation of anemic growth since its "economic bubble" burst in 1990, with real per capita growth averaging just 0.8 percent per year up to 2014.[9] Despite its decidedly unfavorable long-term macroeconomic environment, however, Japan's prime-age male workforce participation has seen far less deterioration than America's over those "lost decades." Between 1990 and 2015, Japan's prime-age male workforce rates slipped by just two percentage points, next to America's five-point drop. The share of prime-age American men neither working nor looking for work is now over two and a half times higher than the Japanese figure. Presumed "cultural" factors (e.g., restricted workforce opportunities for Japanese women) cannot explain away this differential. As we shall see later, workforce participation rates for prime-age women are now higher in Japan than the United States.

Another point worth exploring about the unusual nature of the modern American male's flight from work relates to how strikingly these contrast with the work habits (or work ethic) of the great majority of working-age American men and women who hold down paid jobs.

In theory, we should expect average hours of paid work per employee to decline over time in an increasingly affluent workforce. We have certainly seen this in almost all of today's affluent societies. In the United States, however, a curious aberration has become apparent over the past generation or more: estimated annual hours per U.S. worker have held firm, remaining stuck at a higher level than seen in many countries not yet as wealthy as America today.

Consider the annual hours worked and per capita output over the past generation in the G-7 countries (the world's

FIGURE 4.3. ANNUAL HOURS WORKED PER WORKER VS. GDP PER CAPITA: G-7 COUNTRIES, 1990–2014 PPP (2011 INTERNATIONAL PPP $)

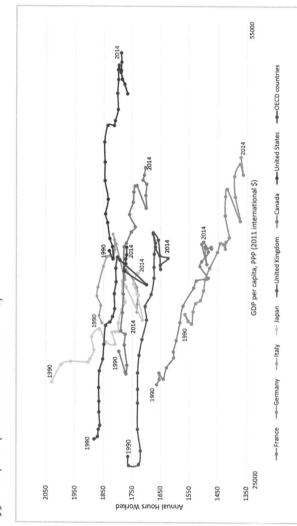

Source: "Average Annual Hours Actually Worked per Worker," OECD.Stat, retrieved on June 21, 2016, https://stats.oecd.org/Index.aspx?DataSetCode=ANHRS; "World Development Indicators," World Bank, retrieved on June 21, 2016, http://databank.worldbank.org/data/reports.aspx?source=world-development-indicators.

major affluent democratic societies: the United States, Japan, Germany, France, Britain, Italy, and Canada; see figure 4.3). No G-7 economy today produces as much value added per citizen as the United States and none have a workforce where employees spend as much of the year on the job.

Japanese employees were once reputed to be workaholics, but over the past generation, average hours of paid work per employee have plummeted: their hours of work are now lower than their U.S. counterparts. Employed Canadians and Britons now work at least one hundred hours per year (over two full workweeks) less than working Yanks. The gap between the United States and France, according to the OECD, is now nearly three hundred hours (over eight full workweeks). More than four hundred annual hours (over ten full workweeks) separate workers in America and Germany.[10] All other G-7 economies report declines in average annual hours along with rising income levels over the past quarter century. Yet the American worker's annual level of hours worked has nearly held constant.

Compare, as well, the annual hours of work per paid employee in G-7 countries with their LFPRs for prime-age men (see figure 4.4). The G-7 countries with lower annual work hours also see somewhat higher percentages of prime-age men altogether absent from the workforce. But America today does not follow this general pattern. Our increasingly productive society simultaneously features stable worker hours per employee—now at levels far higher than other

FIGURE 4.4. PERCENTAGE OF 25–54 MALES OUT OF LABOR FORCE VS. ANNUAL HOURS WORKED PER WORKER, 1991–2014: G–7 COUNTRIES

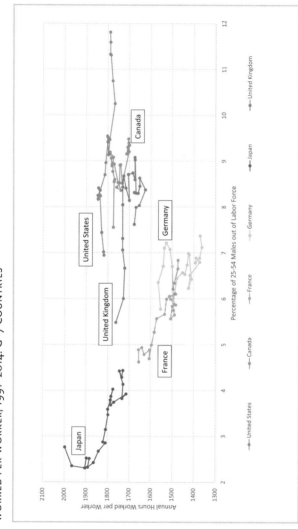

Source: "Average Annual Hours Actually Worked per Worker," OECD.Stat, retrieved on June 21, 2016, https://stats.oecd.org/Index.aspx?DataSetCode=ANHRS; "Labour Force Participation Rate," OECD Data, retrieved on June 21, 2015, https://data.oecd.org/emp/labour-force-participation-rate.htm.

G-7 economies—*and* steadily rising proportions of prime-age men out of the workforce, which are also at levels far higher than other G-7 economies.

It has been over twenty years since Juliet Schor, Boston College professor, coined the phrase "the overworked American,"[11] underscoring our unusual proclivity for long hours and short to nonexistent vacations in relation to our affluent peers abroad. Not generally appreciated, however, is that the land of "the overworked American" is also home to an unusually large and rapidly growing contingent of "underworked Americans": relatively young men who spend absolutely no time at a job and are not acting to alter that situation.

In 1930, John Maynard Keynes famously speculated about life in the future in his "Economic Possibilities for Our Grandchildren."[12] Those grandchildren would most likely be living right about now. In that essay, he dared to predict that the workweek would be much shorter and income levels would be much higher for these future generations. Keynes was correct in the gist of his prophecies: throughout Europe and the rest of the West, income levels are far higher today than when his argument was first published, and the workweek is appreciably shorter (abeit not yet as short as he boldly suggested it might come to be). Yet implicit in Keynes's essay is the assumption that all would share in the spread of free-time in this future world. The notion that some men (and women) would be working the same long hours as their fathers, while a growing caste of prime-age men would be more or less exempt from performing any work at all and supported by the rest of society, as we see in America today, would certainly not have merited mention. That idea would have seemed too absurd and perverse a possibility for serious consideration.

CHAPTER 5

Who Is He? A Statistical Portrait of the Un-Working American Man

≥≤

ALMOST ALL of the collapse of work in adult male America over the past half century is due to the rising numbers of men no longer seeking jobs. Between 1965 and 2015, the employment-to-population ratio for U.S. men twenty and older fell by a bit over thirteen percentage points (81.3 percent to 68.1 percent). Over this same period, LFPRs for U.S. men twenty and over fell by more than twelve percentage points (83.9 percent to 71.5 percent). In effect, exit from the workforce—including retirement—accounted for almost all of the drop in employment levels for all adult men.

The drop in workforce participation rates also accounts for the overwhelming majority of the work rate decline for prime-age men. For men twenty-five–to–fifty-four, work rates dropped by 9.7 percentage points between 1965 and 2015 (94.1 percent to 84.4 percent). Prime-age male LFPRs fell by 8.4 points (96.7 percent to 88.3 percent) over the same time. Consequently, the prime-age male exodus from the labor market accounted for seven-eighths of the total work rate decline. And, unlike withdrawal from the labor force at older ages, a mass workforce exit for prime-of-lifers cannot plausibly be attributed to retirement.

Who are these U.S. men who have left the workforce in their prime working years? In this chapter I will examine their demographic characteristics, as well as some of the key tendencies associated with the steady rapid growth in numbers of this troubling new social group.

Labor markets are fluid and dynamic, characterized by a constant churning. By contrast, there is far less turnover in the pool of un-working prime-age American men. Census Bureau numbers imply that fully two-thirds of those prime-age males who were out of the labor force for any part of 2014 were out of it for the entire year. Thus, while there appears to be some movement both in and out from the ranks of the un-working, checking out of the labor force generally appears to be a long-term proposition for those prime-age men who make the decision not to seek work though they are jobless.

These long-term un-working, or "not in the labor force" (NILF), men are the hard core of modern America's "men without work" problem. According to Bureau of Labor Statistics data, in 2015 an average of 7.2 million prime-age men were NILFs, and the likelihood of being a prime-age American man who neither works nor seeks work was three and a half times greater in 2015 than fifty years earlier (11.7 percent vs. 3.3 percent). But broad trends in the odds of being an un-worker are also apparent for the year 2015 in accordance with a prime-age man's race or ethnicity, educational attainment, marital status and family structure, and nativity (i.e., whether native-born or foreign-born).

With respect to race and ethnicity, the greatest cleavage is between black men and all others, though differences among the huge and diverse nonblack population are also evident. (Hispanic men, for example, were more likely than average to be in a job and out of the NILF pool; the reverse is true for self-identified Native Americans.) According to U.S. race and ethnicity data, however, black males made up nearly twice as much of the prime-age NILF population as prime-age job holders (20.4 percent vs. 10.6 percent). In addition, when Hispanic heritage is thrown into the mix, non-Latino blacks accounted for exactly twice as large a share of prime-age male NILFs as employees (19.8 percent vs. 9.9 percent).

Educational attainment, in turn, dramatically affected the odds that a prime-age male in 2015 would be holding down a job or living as an un-worker. A prime-age man with at least some graduate education was three times more likely to be in the former rather than the latter category. Conversely, men without a high school diploma were more than twice as likely to be among the un-working. With every improvement in educational attainment, the odds of being in the workforce rise. By the same token, the chances of landing in the NILF pool increase the lower the educational attainment. Nevertheless, relatively educated men still accounted for a surprising share of the long-term jobless prime-age men not seeking work. In 2015, over two-fifths of prime-age male un-workers had some college education, and one-sixth had at least a bachelor's degree.

Marital status and family structure/living arrangements likewise prove powerful predictors. Married men accounted for three-fifths of prime-age job holders but only about one-third of NILFs in 2015. On the other hand, men who have never married were underrepresented among the employed and overrepresented among NILFs. (A similar pattern holds for prime-age men who were divorced, separated, or widowed.) Living under the same roof with one or more children also increases the odds of being a worker, regardless of marital status, and married prime-age men with children accounted for over twice as much of the paid workforce as the NILF-force.

Finally, foreign-born men in 2015 were more likely to be job holders and decidedly less likely to be NILFs than the prime-age male population as a whole. Foreign-born males made up more than one-fifth of prime-age job holders in 2015, but less than one-sixth of the un-workers.

In sum, an American man ages twenty-five–to–fifty-four was more likely to be an un-worker in 2015 if he (1) had no more than a high school diploma; (2) was not married and had no children or children who lived elsewhere; (3) was not an immigrant; or (4) was African American.

I will examine the interaction between these factors in a moment. For now, however, I will explore how the role of these factors has changed during the long downward slide in prime-age male LFPRs and how these appreciable changes have influenced this past half-century's male flight from work.

Work rates and LFPRs both have slumped over the past half century for prime-age men of virtually every ethnic group, educational level, and marital status. They have likewise fallen irrespective of family structure for as long as such CPS data have been collected (1968). The only exceptions are foreign-born men. Their work rates and LFPRs actually rose between 1994 and 2015.

By 1965, both prime-age male work rates and LFPRs were already substantially lower for blacks than whites. They also dropped far more steeply for blacks than whites over the next fifty years. It is worth noting, however, that those rates were higher for black men in 1965 than they are for white men today. Additionally, deterioration in labor market performance among prime-age men has been far less pronounced among Latinos than non-Hispanic whites or non-Hispanic blacks since 1971, when the Census Bureau began its annual collection of information on ethnicity for persons of Hispanic heritage.

In 1965, some differential in work and NILF rates were already evident by educational level. Both were lowest among high school dropouts and highest among prime-age men with a college degree. In 1965, however, even high school drop-outs were more likely to be employed and in the workforce than the average U.S. male today. Between 1965 and 2015, work rates for prime-age men with less than a high school degree plummeted by nearly eighteen percentage points, and their inactivity rates shot up by sixteen percentage points. For men with a high school diploma, the work rates fell nearly sixteen points, and NILF rates rose by thirteen points. By contrast, prime-age men with at least some graduate education saw their work rates fall by less than two points and their NILF rates rise by less than two points.

Marital status was already a powerful predictor of American employment behavior in 1965 for prime-age men. A gap of nearly thirteen percentage points separated work rates for the married and the never married; NILF rates were eight points higher for the never married. Even so, LFPRs for these never married in 1965 were somewhat higher than the national average for prime-age men today. Between 1965 and 2015, work rates fell and NILF rates rose for men of every marital status—married, separated, divorced, widowed, and never married—but they worsened far more for the never married.[1]

In 1968, the CPS began asking more detailed questions about family structure. The results track with overall trends for marital status but provide more definition. Work rates in 1968 were nearly twelve points higher for a married man with children than a never-married man without them; LFPRs were a full nine points higher. Over the following decades, labor market performance deteriorated less for married men with children than any other family type.

Though only beginning in 1994, CPS data on employment by nativity are compelling. In 1994, prime-age immigrant men were reportedly less likely to be working than their native-born counterparts and more likely to be out of the labor force altogether. By 2015, this situation had been completely reversed. After two decades of mass immigration, prime-age male work rates were more than five points higher among the foreign born, and LFPRs were over four points higher. Indeed, immigrants pushed national prime-age male work rates and LFPRs up by about one percentage point in 2015.

The long-term fall in prime-age male work rates and rise in NILF rates are also due to the changing weight of subgroups in the composition of the overall population. Over the past half century, America has become more multicultural (less "Anglo"), education attainment has risen sharply, the "traditional" married-with-children family type has sharply declined, and America has become much more foreign born. Our changing racial and ethnic composition does not appear to have had much overall effect on long-term trends in work rates and inactivity rates after adjusting for 1965 ethnicity weightings. America's prime-age male work rate would have been about half a percentage point lower in 2015 and the prime-age male inactivity level three-tenths of a point lower.

No change at all in 2015 work rates and LFPRs would come from substituting 1971 population weightings for race and Hispanic origin. Broadly speaking, the relatively unfavorable trends for prime-age male African Americans are largely offset by the relatively favorable trends among Latinos over these decades.

On the other hand, changes in prime-age males' educational makeup have had a big effect on work rates and inactivity rates—a strongly positive effect. If 1965 distribution of educational attainments for prime-age men still applied, the work rate would be nearly six additional percentage points lower and the NILF rate four percentage points higher than they actually were in 2015. In brief, the collapse of work for modern America's men happened *despite* considerable upgrades in educational attainment in recent decades.

If educational attainment has buoyed work rates and workforce participation for prime-age American men, changes in marriage patterns and family structure had at least as strong an influence in pulling those rates down. In 1965, 85 percent of prime-age men were married, nearly thirty percentage points higher than 2015. On the other hand, the proportion of never-married men was over three times higher in 2015 than 1965. With 1965 proportions of married/separated or divorced/widowed/never-married men, our prime-age male 2015 work rate would have been over six percentage points higher. The NILF rate would have been at least six points lower—less than one-half of its actual 2015 level. Adjustments for family structure and at-home children point in the same direction, although neither is as strong.

Interestingly, adjustment for nativity suggests work rates would have been four percentage points lower in 2015 with 1994 ratios of prime-age men who are immigrant to native born. At the same time, prime-age male inactivity rates would have been only slightly higher (0.3 percentage points). How could this be? Between the early 1990s and today, reported work rates for prime-age male immigrants went up while the unemployment rate went down. Thus, the overall LFPRs in our hypothetical alternative 2015 were scarcely impacted.

This brief demographic sketch of the modern American un-worker suggests that powerful social influences shape whether a prime-age male will have a job or be in the work-force at all and that these social influences have changed significantly over the last fifty years. Such a formulation, however, runs perilously close to the social determinist fallacy—the assumption that humans are helpless objects at the mercy of overarching social forces, without agency in affecting their life outcomes.

Of course, human beings are endowed with free will. Their lives are not merely an unending series of readings from socioeconomic probability functions. People can make choices about their lives. Obviously, they hardly have a choice about their ethnicity or race, but they have some choice about their educational attainment (although some will debate just how much choice the disadvantaged truly possess). What is incontestable, however, is that people have immense choice in two realms of social identity: whether they marry (and to a lesser but not an inconsiderable degree, whether they have children and/or stay married) and whether they move to America from another country. Such volitional behavior is at least as important as seeming social forces in explaining work patterns for America men today.

No matter their race or educational status, married men raising a family work more, and never-married men without children or children in their home work less. No matter their ethnicity or race, prime-age men who come to this country work more than those here by birth. Neither a wedding ring nor a green card confers innate advantage in the competition for jobs. Rather, marriage and migration decisions point to motivations, aspirations, priorities, values, and other intangibles that do so much to explain real-world human achievements.

Consider race and ethnicity. America today is not a wholly colorblind society, even if it is much closer to this ideal than it was fifty years ago. The legacy of prejudice might seem to explain why prime-age male work rates and workforce participation rates are lower for blacks than whites today. But they cannot explain why work rates and LFPRs for white men today are decidedly lower than they were for black men in 1965. And they surely cannot explain why prime-age male LFPRs today are higher for Latinos than non-Hispanic whites (see figure 5.1). Nor can they explain why labor participation rates of married black men twenty-five-to–fifty-four are

FIGURE 5.1. U.S. MALE (25–54) NON-INSTITUTIONAL CIVILIAN LABOR FORCE PARTICIPATION RATES BY ETHNICITY: HISPANIC VS. NON-HISPANIC WHITE, 1994–2015

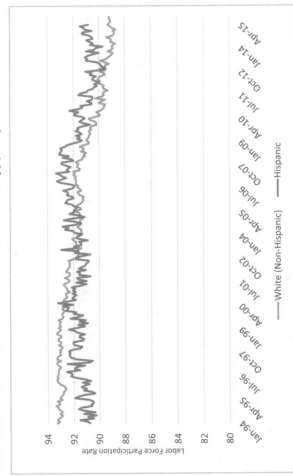

Note: Series break for ethnicity after December 2002; for race after December 1995, December 2002, and April 2012.

Source: "Bureau of Labor Statistics, Current Population Survey, January 1994–September 2015," DataFerrett, retrieved on October 8, 2015.

FIGURE 5.2. LABOR FORCE PARTICIPATION RATE FOR MEN AGES 25–54 BY MARITAL STATUS AND RACE: MARRIED BLACK VS. NEVER-MARRIED WHITE

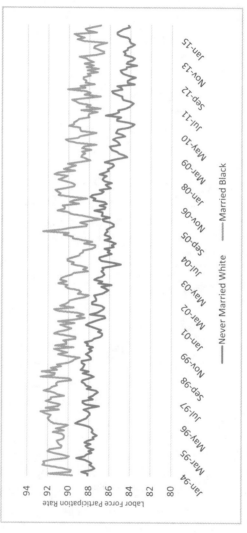

Note: Series break for race after December 1995, December 2002, and April 2012.

Source: "Bureau of Labor Statistics, Current Population Survey, January 1994–September 2015," DataFerrett, retrieved on October 20, 2015.

higher than for never-married white men in that same age group (see figure 5.2).

Next, consider education. It is widely accepted today that educational attainment is determinative of labor force prospects. As important as the advantages of education surely are, however, behavior and choice also affect labor market outcomes for men with any given level of education attainment. Prime-age LFPRs today for married men with only high school diplomas, for example, are distinctly higher than for never-married men with some college education or an associate degree (see figure 5.3). Similarly, among prime-age men with less than a high school degree, 2015 LFPRs were roughly twenty percentage points higher for the married than the never married. Indeed, LFPRs for contemporary prime-age American men are essentially indistinguishable for married high school dropouts and never-married college graduates (see figure 5.4).

As for nativity, today's foreign-born prime-age men are more likely to have a job or be in the labor force than their native-born counterparts. This is true for every major ethnic group. In 2015, foreign-born prime-age men outperformed their native-born counterparts in LFPRs by nearly three percentage points among white Americans, over three points among Asian Americans, and a striking ten points among black Americans. The LFPR was also six percentage points higher for foreign-born prime Latino males than for native-born prime-age Latino males.

FIGURE 5-3. LABOR FORCE PARTICIPATION RATE FOR MEN AGES 25–54 BY MARITAL STATUS AND EDUCATIONAL ATTAINMENT: NEVER MARRIED WITH SOME COLLEGE OR ASSOCIATE DEGREE VS. MARRIED HIGH SCHOOL GRADUATE

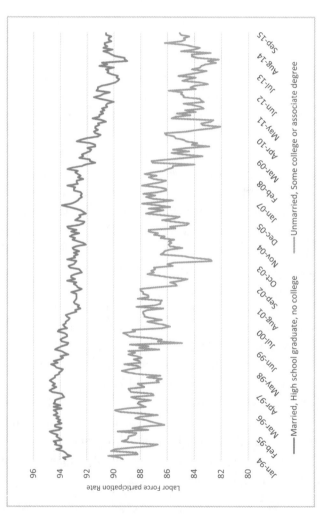

Source: "Bureau of Labor Statistics, Current Population Survey, January 1994–September 2015," DataFerrett, retrieved on October 20, 2015.

FIGURE 5.4. LABOR FORCE PARTICIPATION RATE FOR MEN AGES 25–54 BY MARITAL STATUS AND EDUCATIONAL ATTAINMENT: NEVER MARRIED WITH BACHELOR'S DEGREE OR HIGHER VS. MARRIED HIGH SCHOOL DROPOUT

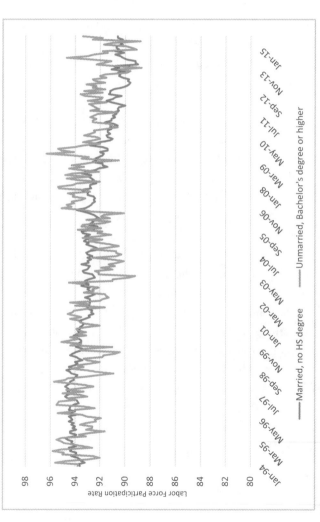

Source: "Bureau of Labor Statistics, Current Population Survey, January 1994–September 2015," DataFerrett, retrieved on October 20, 2015.

Further, immigrants have greater LFPRs than native-born Americans today at every level of educational standing, with the curious exception of college graduates. For prime-age men with some college, the foreign-born edge in LFPRs in 2015 was less than one percentage point. But for those with high school diplomas but no college, immigrant rates were nearly eight percentage points higher. For those without a high school diploma, the difference was an astonishing twenty-five percentage points (92 versus 67 percent).[2] Foreign high school dropouts today have LFPRs close to the highly advantaged cohort of native-born male college graduates, with whom they arguably have little in common, save their exceedingly low odds of being out of the workforce (see figure 5.5).

For the most part, the foreign-born high school dropouts are Latino—many with limited English language ability and many who entered the United States illegally. Despite "living in the shadows," they largely seem to have had no difficulty becoming part of the U.S. labor force. One critical determinant to being in the U.S. workforce today seems to be wanting to be there in the first place.

FIGURE 5.5. LABOR FORCE PARTICIPATION RATES FOR MEN 25–54 BY NATIVITY AND EDUCATIONAL ATTAINMENT: NATIVE BORN WITH COLLEGE DEGREE OR MORE VS. FOREIGN BORN WITH LESS THAN HIGH SCHOOL DIPLOMA

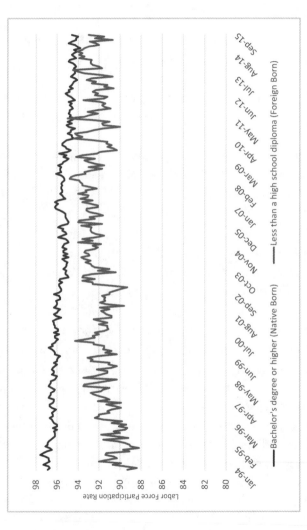

Source: "Bureau of Labor Statistics, Current Population Survey, January 1994–September 2015," DataFerrett, retrieved on October 20, 2015.

CHAPTER 6

Idle Hands: Time Use, Social Participation, and the Male Flight from Work

———————— ⋛⋚ ————————

FREE-TIME MAY be a luxury good in universal demand, but it does not necessarily follow that such luxery will universally be put to good use by those who obtain it.

Successive generations in our consumer era appear to be ever less aware of the age-old distinction between leisure and idleness in the spending of free-time. Bluntly stated, leisure refines and elevates; idleness corrupts and degrades.

Free-time can be devoted to recreation, reflection, and self-improvement as well as the pursuit of knowledge, spirituality, and the arts. A respite from toil and chores is a prerequisite for contemplation and the deepening of consciousness that allows for cultural advance. Indeed in the words of German philosopher Josef Pieper's probing treatise, leisure is the basis of culture.[1]

Free-time can also be wasted or expended in ways that diminish the individual and his bonds to family and community. A predilection for character- and capability-diminishing whiles was once an occasion for explicit opprobrium, not only because these habits were held to constitute personal flaws, but also because they were understood to risk untoward social consequences.

A number of religious traditions have long held that such idleness imperiled one's soul. Roman Catholic doctrine condemns "sloth," a state of woeful inactivity and avoidance of temporal and eternal obligations deemed a cardinal sin. Protestant theologians have tended to be even harder on idleness than their Catholic brethren. As Max Weber famously noted, the Protestant ethic maintained that "waste of time is thus the first and in principle the deadliest of sins."[2]

Not so long ago, even secular reformers identified "idleness" as one of the great social ills that enlightened government policy in Western countries should address. Lord William Beveridge, whose 1942 "Beveridge Report" provided wartime Britain with its initial blueprint for the postwar British welfare state, enumerated five "Giant Evils" that social policy should confront. One was idleness. "Idleness is not the same as Want," he explained, "It is a positive separate evil from which men do not escape by having an income. . . . Idleness even on an income corrupts."[3] He specifically targeted "Freedom from Idleness" as one of the great social objectives that postwar policy should strive to achieve.

How time is allocated is not wholly immaterial to the character formation of individuals or the balance of vice and virtue in a society. So how does the un-working prime-age man—with more free-time on his hands than other males or females in the United States today, or perhaps any contemporaries in American history—make use of his luxury?

I begin by examining the reported time use and social participation patterns of U.S. men between the ages of twenty-five and fifty-four who neither worked nor sought work for at least twelve months.

According to the Census Bureau's CPS Annual Social and Economic Survey (ASEC), 68 percent of prime-age men out of the workforce for any part of 2014 were out for the entire year. ASEC data on this trend go back at least twenty years. In 1994, only about half of prime-age men out of work for any part of the year were out for the entire year. The fraction has been gradually rising over time (except for a slight decline after the sharp spike in the wake of the post–Great Recession spike in 2011). These figures suggest that once a prime-age man removes himself from the labor force, there is a good —and increasing—chance he will remain an un-worker for a long time.

According to responses to this ASEC annual survey, about 15 percent of the prime-age men who did not work at all in 2014 stated they were unemployed because they could not find work. In other words, five out of six prime-age men gave reasons other than a lack of jobs for their absence from the workplace. Twenty years earlier, 16 percent of men not working the whole of 1994 said the reason was an inability to find a job. After the 2008 crash, that share shot up to 28 percent in 2009, the highest such reading reported over the past two decades. But even in that economic *annus horribilis*, well over 70 percent of the prime-age men out of work that whole year said the reason was something other than an inability to find work.

For a twenty-year period (1994–2014), the average annual share of prime-age men who said they were not at work all year because they were unable to find a job was 14 percent. And the ASEC survey, unlike the Bureau of Labor Statistics numbers, does not distinguish between those who have left the labor force altogether and the long-term unemployed still seeking work in the total number of persons out of the workforce for the whole year. Since the long-term unemployed are by definition looking for jobs, this means that the 15 percent figure for the year 2014 actually overstates—perhaps appreciably—the fraction of NILF men out of work because they are having trouble finding a job—and a longer term average as well.

Other Census Bureau surveys provide additional information on the reason men say they have been without jobs for relatively long periods of time. One is the Survey of Income and Program Participation (SIPP). In 2001 and 2007, Census Bureau researchers used SIPP data (from 1996 and 2004, respectively) to examine the demographic profiles of adults fifteen and older who had been without jobs for four consecutive months and the reasons they gave for nonemployment.

For the broad twenty–to–sixty-four age group, just 13 percent of nonworking men gave "unable to find work" as the reason for not working in 1996. In 2004, the corresponding proportion was 14 percent. Once again, lack of job opportunities is identified by only a small minority of men without work as the reason for being without employment. Since this example of nonworkers includes not only the long-term unemployed but also those on short-term unemployment, the rate for NILF men must be even smaller.

The SIPP surveys permit us to tease out one bit of information on nonworking men that we cannot obtain from ASEC those who say they did not work over the past four consecutive months because they were caring for children or others. In 1996, the fraction of such men twenty–to–sixty-four was a mere 2.6 percent, compared to nearly 39 percent for nonworking women of the same age.[4] In 2004, the reported share was 2.4 percent for men and nearly 39 percent for women.[5] For the year 2013, SIPP microdata indicate that only a slightly higher fraction of prime-age men—just 4.6 percent—said they were out of the labor force because they were looking after a child or someone else.

These stark numbers plainly suggest that un-working men in modern America simply do not prioritize care for children or other family members. And this vast "care chasm" separating un-working men and un-working women cannot entirely, or even mainly, be explained by differences in family type or structure.

What, then, do today's un-working prime-age men do with all their free-time? What do they do from the moment they wake up in the morning until the moment they fall asleep at night? Our best aperture into these patterns is the Bureau of Labor Statistics (BLS) annual American Time Use Survey (ATUS), conducted annually since 2003.[6] In this survey, respondents report how they have used their time over the twenty-four-hour day just completed. Its main objective is to enrich our understanding of daily work patterns by Americans. But the survey also attempts to elicit considerable detail on the amount of time spent sleeping, eating, and engaging in other activities.

Some researchers have used the ATUS and earlier time-use surveys to measure broad changes in postwar America's patterns of work and free-time use. In a number of studies, for example, Mark Aguiar and Eric Hurst examined the weekly hours that adult men and women devoted to work and nonwork between 1965 and 2005.[7] They estimated that between 1965 and 2005, weekly nonwork[8] rose by about eight hours per week for men without high school degrees, while it fell by over two hours per week for those men with a college degree or more. Most of this movement came between 1985 and 2003–5. By the dawn of the twenty-first century, they found, men without high school degrees were enjoying over thirteen more nonwork hours per week than their college-educated counterparts. By 2003–5, more educated men were spending about five more hours a week at paid work than the less educated (high school degree or less), but they were also spending more time doing home chores and caring for kids.

The curious increase in what Aguiar and Hurst termed

"leisure inequality" requires some explanation, since their findings seem to fly in the face of the strong worldwide tendency for work time to decline as income and wealth increase. They show that part of the recent increase in "leisure inequality" was due to the increasing numbers of un-working men rather than unemployed or underemployed men. But this was only part of the story. While they calculated that the overwhelming increase in nonwork time for less-educated men was attributable to declining work rates, they also found that more educated men (beyond a high school education) were spending more time clocking in a greater number of overall weekly hours at the job, doing home chores, and caring for children than two decades earlier. They concluded that,

> One possible explanation of the unequal response is that the preference for leisure (the disutility of work) increased more for low-educated workers during this time. This explanation is consistent with the fact that individuals of differing educational attainment who are out of the labor market and facing the same prices exhibit dramatically different time allocation decisions.[9]

In other words, these anomalous patterns may largely have been driven by a change in preferences or tastes, especially on the part of men without jobs and particularly among less-educated men without jobs.

A closer examination of reported time-use patterns brings the differences in tastes and preferences for men with and without jobs into sharper focus. Thanks to the relatively detailed breakdowns of time use by reported activity, we can get a surprisingly comprehensive picture of the differences in the daily routines for prime-age employed and unemployed men and men who neither have jobs nor are seeking work.

There are two intrinsic shortcomings to such self-reported chronicles of personal activity. The first is inaccurate or inattentive recall.[10] The second is the potential reluctance of respondents to attest even in an ostensibly confidential interview or written diary to behavior that might seem to contravene social norms. The ATUS has made diligent efforts to deal with both problems, but they're there.

Working prime-age women offer an instructive comparison with un-working men because they tend to be especially pressed by "time poverty."[11] In addition to their work obligations, most of these women are also raising children. In 2015, 66 percent of employed women ages twenty-five to fifty-four lived in households with at least one child under eighteen. This compared with just 37 percent of prime-age NILF men.[12] Given their manifold commitments, these working women tend to be the major demographic group with the least discretionary time at their disposal. They thus offer an informative counterpoint to NILF men, who have more discretionary time than any other major demographic group of working-age adults.

The differences in these time-use profiles are stunning (see table 6.1). Patterns for all groups changed little between the first annual ATUS survey in 2003 and the most recent as of this writing (2014). We can therefore concentrate on profiles from the year 2014. Not surprisingly, the two greatest differences in reported time use among these four groups were in "work and work-related activities" on the one hand, and "socializing, relaxing, and leisure" on the other.

Employed prime-age men reportedly spent an average of about six hours a day (including weekends and holidays), or 2,200 hours a year, on work and work-related activity. Employed women spent about five hours a day, or 1,850 hours a year. Unemployed prime-age men averaged over an hour a day, or about four hundred hours a year, on these activities (mainly job search). Prime-age NILF men averaged seven minutes a day on such activities, or about forty-three hours a year.

Without work, work travel, or job search to attend to, these nonworkforce men gained an extra 2,150 hours of free-time each year against men with a job; more than 1,800 hours a year against women with a job, and an extra 350 more free-time hours against the men who were unemployed but looking for work. What is striking, however, is how little of this enormous free-time dividend was devoted to helping others in their family or community. In 2014, for example, NILF men spent no more time engaged in household care than employed women and less than unemployed men. NILF men also spent appreciably less time caring for other household members than employed women or unemployed men and no more than working men. NILF males spent two minutes more

Table 6.1. Reported Time Use by Selected Activities: Prime-Age (25–54) Men and Women by Employment Status, 2014 (Average Minutes per Day)

Activity	Men Not in Labor Force	Employed Men	Unemployed Men	Employed Women
Personal Care (Including Sleep)	608	532	577	564
Household Care	109	78	114	109
Caring for Household Members	28	28	47	47
Work	7	363	68	305
Education	25	4	47	8
Eating or Drinking	62	64	60	59
Socializing, Relaxing, and Leisure	472	221	353	191

Source: "American Time Use Survey, United States Department of Labor, Bureau of Labor Statistics, 2014," retrieved on July 29, 2016.

a day caring for nonhousehold members than employed men but eight minutes a day less than unemployed males. Finally, these men without work men spent less time in religious and volunteer activities than any of the three other groups.

On the other hand, NILF men spent more time in 2014 on "personal care"—sleeping, grooming, health-related self-care, and the like—totaling some 200 more hours each year than unemployed men, 250 hours more than working women, and over 450 hours a year more than men with jobs. Yet the greatest difference in the daily routine of un-working men compared to the other three groups was, of course, the time spent on "socializing, relaxing, and leisure." Un-working men reportedly devoted nearly eight hours a day to these activities. Compared to other demographic groups, NILF men reportedly expended over seven hundred more hours each year than unemployed men, fifteen hundred more hours than men with jobs, and a staggering seventeen hundred more hours than working women in this category of "socializing, relaxing, and leisure."[13] In effect this was akin to a full-time job for the average un-working prime-age man.

Just what leisure-based activities are these un-working men doing eight hours a day? Among Americans twenty-five–to–fifty-four, men who neither worked nor sought work in 2014 spent more time engaging in the following categories than working men and women or unemployed men: "attending gambling establishments," "tobacco and drug use," "listening to the radio," and "arts and (perhaps incongruously) crafts as a hobby."

On an annualized basis, un-working men spent about seventy hours more time "socializing and communicating with others" than unemployed men, nearly one hundred hours more than employed women, and over one hundred hours more than working men. When it came to "television and movies (not religious)," the contrast between NILF men and all the rest was so enormous that it suggests a fundamental difference in mentality. For un-working men, watching TV and movies ate up an average of five and a half hours a day. That's four hours a day more than for working women, nearly three and a half hours more than working men, and a striking two hours a day more than *unemployed* men.

And what exactly are the un-working prime-age men doing during these many hours that account for so much of their daily routine? The ATUS does not allow us to determine this. It is a reasonable inference, however, that the Internet may play a big role here, through desktops, hand-held devices, and so forth.[14] Whatever they're viewing or doing on their big screens, computers, or smartphones, it must be alluring. Between the 2003 and 2014 ATUS surveys, time spent on "socializing, relaxing, and leisure" declined slightly for prime-age unemployed men, as well as prime-age workers of both sexes. It jumped by just over half an hour a day for un-working prime-age men (nearly two hundred hours a year). NILF men "funded" the increase in such activities by reducing other allocations in their daily time budget. Reductions in time devoted to volunteering, religious activities, and purposeful movement outside the house ("travel"), for example, reportedly freed up almost exactly the amount of time newly applied to "socializing, relaxing and leisure."

Earlier I mentioned that about a tenth of the prime-age men neither working nor seeking work are pursuing education. Since it seemed reasonable to suspect that these motivated adult students might have different patterns of time use than the great majority of prime-age NILFs, I disaggregated the overall NILF population into adult students and NEETs (those who are neither employed nor in education/training; see table 6.2). Adult students reported spending about thirty hours a week studying. They spent much less time on "socializing, relaxing, and leisure" than unemployed men, although more than employed men. They devoted less time to "eating/drinking" than any other group and more time doing home chores ("household care" plus "household services") than NEETs. They also spent much more time volunteering—more time, in fact, than any other group—though they spent less time caring for others than any other group—perhaps a result of their household and living arrangements.

Prime-age NEET men, on the other hand, spent even less time volunteering than the NILF averages suggest—and significantly more time on "socializing, relaxing, and leisure." To those assorted activities, they devoted a reported average of over eight hours a day, or almost three thousand hours a year. Paramount here is "television and movies (not religious)," which consumes an average of nearly six hours of the prime-age NEET man's day, or 2,100 hours a year. Adult students, by contrast, reportedly spent about four hours a day watching TV and movies—about the same as for men with jobs.

The General Social Survey (GSS), a large-scale and ongo-

Table 6.2. Reported Time Use by Selected Activities for NILF Prime-Age Men (25–54): Adult Students vs. Neither Employed Nor in Education and Training (NEETs), 2014 (Average Minutes per Day)

MEN NOT IN THE LABOR FORCE (2014)		
ACTIVITY	**NEET**	**IN SCHOOL (ADULT STUDENTS)**
Personal Care	607	619
Work	7	0
Education	5	261
Eating or Drinking	63	55
Socializing or Leisure	489	276
Sports	25	8
Religious	4	4
Volunteering	2	17
Travel	40	63

Source: "American Time Use Survey, United States Department of Labor, Bureau of Labor Statistics, 2014," available at http://www.bls.gov/tus/datafiles_2014.ht. Retrieved on July 29, 2016.

ing sociological study administered by the National Opinion Research Center, allows us to examine self-reported patterns of social engagement, social participation, and asocial behavior for prime-age U.S. men by employment status.[15] By every indicator, men not in the workforce look to be less socially engaged than men with work (though by some of these indicators they do not appear less engaged than the unemployed).

There is a longstanding pattern of lower religious attendance for nonworking men than for working men twenty-five–to–fifty-five. Between 1972 and 2014, formal worship was on the decline among all American adults, but the proportion of un-working men who never went to worship was distinctly higher than for men with work. No appreciable difference existed, however, in nonattendance for un-workers and the unemployed. Un-working men were likewise less likely to have volunteered over the previous month than working men. And while newspaper readership has declined for all Americans since the 1970s, daily newspaper reading was appreciably lower for the un-working than the working, despite having more free-time. Working men were also consistently more likely to vote in presidential election years than un-working men.

Finally, the GSS reveals a sharp divide between working men and other prime-age groups with respect to self-reported illegal drug use (see figure 6.1). In 2004 (the most recent year for such information), 8 percent of working men and 22 percent of unemployed men reported some illegal drug use over the past year, while nearly one in three (31 percent) of prime-age male un-workers admitted to illegal drug use.

I have not attempted to adjust these ATUS and GSS results for ethnicity, educational attainment, marital status, or other characteristics. A more nuanced picture may emerge from such refinements. I hope others will pursue this work. I should point out that in the GSS, a number of social participation and social engagement indicators are not appreciably different for men who have no job but are looking for one and the jobless men who are not seeking work. Yet the overall picture of the daily life rhythms of prime-age men who have made a long-term exit from the workforce is distinctive.

To a distressing degree, these men appear to have relinquished what we think of ordinarily as adult responsibilities not only as breadwinners but as parents, family members, community members, and citizens. Having largely freed themselves of such obligations, they fill their days in the pursuit of more immediate sources of gratification. While a minority (those in training or further education) can be seen as pursuing or already possessing a vocation in life, the vast majority cannot be so described. On the contrary, the data here suggest that something like infantilization besets some un-working men.

These data raise troubling questions about the suitability of these long-term un-workers for reentry into the workplace. In the wake of the 2008 crash, some economic research has focused on the "duration dependence" of unemployment—

FIGURE 6.1. Percentage Reporting Illegal Drug Use in the Last Year by Work Status: U.S. Men Ages 25–54 (GSS 2004)

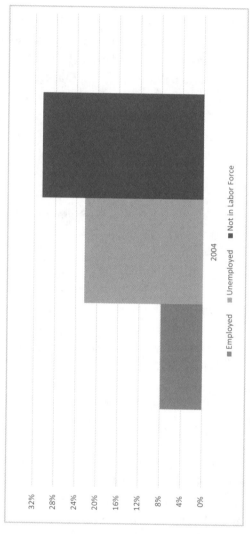

Note: Labor Status: employed (working full time, working part time), unemployed (temporarily not working, unemployed laid off), not in labor force (keeping house, retired, school, other)

Source: "General Social Survey, NORC at the University of Chicago," GSS Data Explorer, retrieved on November 24, 2015, https://gssdataexplorer.norc.org/.

the extent to which being out of work for a relatively long time itself makes it harder for a would-be worker to secure a job, all other things being equal.[16] In one study, prospective real-world employers were sent over three thousand fictional resumes for male job applicants. The imaginary candidates were identical in demographic, education, and skill characteristics, but some had longer or shorter spells out of the workforce.[17] This experiment found that employers across a wide range of fields and occupations were much more reluctant to offer an interview to a man who had been out of a job more than six months. These striking findings prompted wide discussion, leading some to talk of employer "discrimination" and others to speculate about the possible perceived atrophy of job skills among men without work.

We should not put too much weight on a single study. But that paper helps frame an intriguing question, as does an enormous real-world experiment the United States has already conducted. We know that certain Americans who had been out of the workforce for many years—or only first attempted to enter the workforce in their thirties or forties— did find employment in the modern workplace, and did so by the tens of millions. These Americans are called women— and, more specifically, most were called mothers. Regardless of previous job experience, a mother who has raised children typically develops a number of skills that are valued (and arguably indispensable) in the workplace: among them, reliability and dependability in following a schedule. Whatever their other putative shortcomings, these mothers who were in charge of infants and young children were seldom idle. Can the same can be said today of the prime-age American man who has neither worked nor looked for work for six months, a year, or even longer?

CHAPTER 7

Long-Term Structural Forces and the Decline of Work for American Men

꘎

THUS FAR I have examined the dimensions of the collapse of work for men over the past half century, the role of the ongoing flight from work in this collapse, the poor LFPRs today of U.S. men in relation to those in other affluent Western countries, the changing sociodemographic characteristics of the American man who is neither working nor looking for work, and the time-use and social participation patterns of the un-working American man. Our examination of modern America's "men without work" problem, however, has yet to touch upon the role of momentous changes in the postwar U.S. economy in exacerbating this problem—or perhaps in creating it altogether.

Any account of America's growing male work problem that does not recognize that macroeconomic changes have played a part in this troubling dynamic cannot help but be incomplete. Therefore, it's important to summarize some of the thinking and evidence suggesting that long-term structural forces (including such things as international trade, technological and financial innovation, outsourcing, the rise of the on-demand economy, temporary work, and other trends shaping aggregate demand) may be responsible for much, if not most, of the decline in work for men in postwar America.

A 2016 report by the president's Council of Economic Advisers (CEA) did a good job of laying out this case.[1] After documenting the long-term decline in prime-age male work-force participation rates and sorting out some of its compo-nents, the report rightly suggested that these long-term labor force trends can be explained in terms of three different kinds of effect: (1) supply side, (2) demand side, and (3) institu-tional. This chapter will focus on the demand-side effect.

Structural and macroeconomic forces would be demand-side explanations for declining employment rates and workforce participation. The CEA report offered a careful presentation of the demand-side explanation, focusing par-ticularly on the evidence for decreasing demand for less-skilled labor in postwar America:

> If less-educated men were simply choosing to work less . . . this should raise the relative wages of the less-educated men who choose to continue participating in the workforce. Yet, in recent decades the opposite has happened: less-educated Americans have actu-ally suffered a reduction in their wages relative to other groups.
>
> A number of studies have identified declining

labor market opportunities for low-skilled workers and related stagnant real wage growth as the most likely explanation for the decline of prime-age male labor force participation, at least for the period in the mid- to late 1970s and 1980s. . . . More recently, economists have suggested that a relative decline in labor demand for occupations that are middle-skilled or middle-paying may have begun contributing to the decline in participation in the 1990s . . . As demand for these middle-skilled workers has fallen, they may have displaced lower-skilled workers from their lower-skilled jobs . . . leading some lower-skilled workers to leave the labor force . . .

Possible causes include technological advances and globalization, including import competition and offshoring . . . Some economists point to "skill-biased technological change": advances that benefit workers with certain skill sets more than others . . . These forces have, among other things, eliminated large numbers of American manufacturing jobs over a number of decades . . . leaving many people—mostly men—unable to find new ones.[2]

This passage presents the consensus view among contemporary economists on the dynamics of these "demand-side" forces. Most economists would agree that these structural and macroeconomic changes have depressed demand for labor, especially for less-educated, lower-skilled labor in the postwar era.

I concur with this assessment and would further add that other macroeconomic factors less emphasized in the CEA report—such as the U.S. economy's relatively disappointing record in generating economic growth since the start of the new century—have also limited demand for work. The question, however, is how significant an impact these "demand-side" factors have had on the collapse of work for American men. We cannot hope to settle that question here, but we can review some of the evidence suggesting that the impact of such structural and macro-economic changes may have been more qualified than some believe.

First, there is a remarkably steady decline in LFPRs for prime-age U.S. men over the past fifty years. This decline has now proceeded with nearly clocklike regularity, almost totally uninfluenced by the business cycle, for half a century

Notes: Gray columns indicate recessions. Recession variables: The data used to create this figure are from the Current Population Survey (CPS) and were downloaded from the Bureau of Labor Statistics. The data used to create the regression table in the upper left corner are also from the Current Population Survey but were downloaded from IPUMS-CPS for statistical manipulation. 1 if "year" variable falls into any time during the following list of recession dates; 0 otherwise.

Recession dummy variables for the following recessions spanning the subsequent years: 1969–1970, 1973–1975, 1980–1982, 1990–1991, 2001, and 2007–2009.

Sources: "Labor Force Statistics from the Current Population Survey: Men 25–54 from 1948–2015 (Monthly Data)," Bureau of Labor Statistics, http://data.bls.gov/pdq/querytool.jsp?survey=ln; "U.S. Business Cycle Expansions and Contractions," Recession Data: National Bureau of Economic Research (NBER), http://www.nber.org/cycles .html.

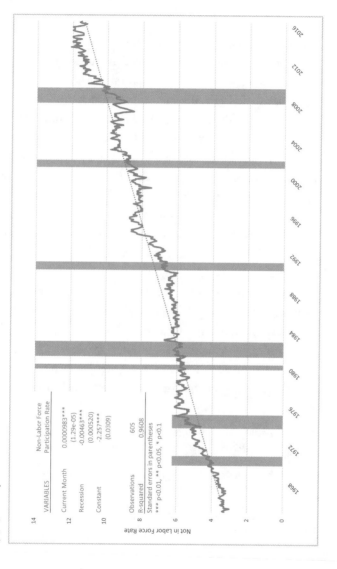

FIGURE 7.1. RATE OF NON–LABOR FORCE PARTICIPATION FROM U.S. MALES 25–54 YEARS OF AGE, (1965–2016)

VARIABLES	Non–Labor Force Participation Rate
Current Month	0.0000983***
	(1.29e-05)
Recession	-0.00463***
	(0.000520)
Constant	-2.257***
	(0.0309)
Observations	605
R-squared	0.9608

Standard errors in parentheses
*** $p<0.01$, ** $p<0.05$, * $p<0.1$

(see figure 7.1). America suffered seven recessions between 1965 and 2015, but knowing when these recessions occurred gives us no additional information on the trajectory of the prime-age male LFPR decline. (If fact, it actually looks as if recessions may slightly *slow* the flight from work.) By the same token, knowing whether the U.S. economy was growing rapidly or slowly or, for that matter, contracting provides almost no help in anticipating the pace at which prime-age men would be leaving the labor force. Sociologists and economists once remarked on the curious and counterintuitive nature of this trajectory and presumed it would have to be reversed.[3] Today they accept it as a fact of life.[4] As Alan Kruger, Princeton economist and former chairman of the Council of Economic Advisers for President Obama, remarked in a speech in 2015, "According to CPS data, the monthly rate for transitioning from out of the labor force to back in the labor force is unrelated to the business cycle."[5]

Second, unlike LFPRs, work rates for U.S. men (including prime-age men) fell in recessions and stabilized in recoveries.

Note: Gray columns indicate recession start and end dates.

Sources: Recession data start and end dates are determined by the National Bureau of Economic Research (NBER) according to "U.S. Business Cycle Expansions and Contractions," Recession Data: National Bureau of Economic Research (NBER), http://www.nber.org/cycles.html.

Labor force participation data were generated by "Labor Force Statistics from the Current Population Survey," Men LNS12300001, Women LNS12300002, Bureau of Labor Statistics, retrieved on August 5, 2016, http://data.bls.gov/pdq/querytool.jsp?survey=ln.

FIGURE 7.2. WORK RATES FOR MEN AND WOMEN AGES 25–54: UNITED STATES, 1965–2015

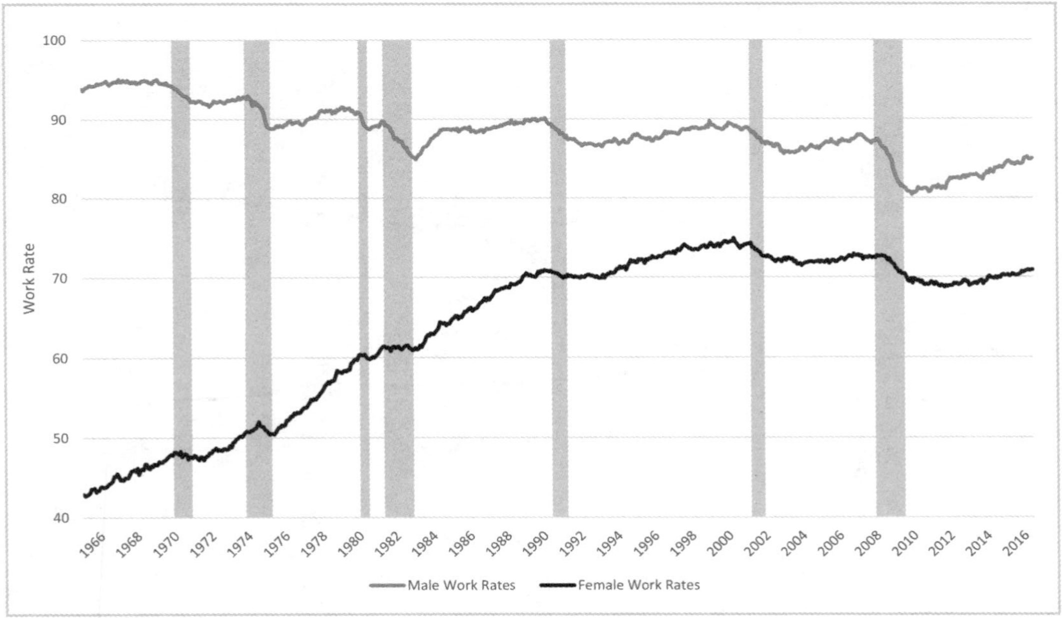

FIGURE 7.3. LABOR FORCE PARTICIPATION RATES FOR MEN AND WOMEN AGES 25–54: JAPAN VS. THE UNITED STATES, 1990–2015

But work rates for women seem less affected—and in some recessions seem basically unaffected (see figure 7.2). Between 1965 and the late 1990s—over the course of five recessions—prime-age female work rates rose by a cumulative total of over thirty percentage points. It remains to be explained what sort of structural or macroeconomic "demand-side effect" would impact labor demand for only half the U.S. population.

Third, slow growth does not necessarily make for weak labor demand in affluent modern economies (see figure 7.3). Despite a much weaker growth rate, Japan had much stronger labor force participation numbers than the United States even in the "lost decades" of the 1990s, when the U.S. economy was growing robustly. And Japan's more favorable LFPR trends cannot be written off as a "cultural" anomaly explained by unusually low LFPRs for Japanese women. On the contrary, Japanese female rates rose steadily and, in fact, now exceed U.S. rates for prime-age women.

Notes: The Japanese labor force participation rate is referred to as the "activity rate." Only annual data was available for females in Japan ages 25–54. Monthly "activity rate" data for males in Japan ages 25–54 were averaged to create an annual "activity rate."

Sources: "Japanese and United States Labor Force Participation Rates," LRAc25FE-JPA156N, FRED, https://fred.stlouisfed.org/series/LRAC25FEJPA156N;

"Activity Rate: Aged 25–54 Males From Japan," LRA 25MAJPM156S; "Activity Rate: Aged 25–54 Females in Japan," LRAC25FEJPA156N; "Activity Rate: Aged 25–54 Males in The United States," LRAC25MAUSM156N; "Activity Rate: Aged 25–54 Females in The United States," LRAC25FEUSM156N.

Fourth, not all less-educated prime-age men in America were subject to the negative labor market demand-side effect. A comparison of LFPRs for native-born and foreign-born lower-skilled men of prime working age makes this clear (see figure 7.4). By 2015, the gap between LFPRs for such native and immigrant men without high school degrees was over twenty-four percentage points. Between 1994 and 2015, LFPRs for these native-born prime-age men plunged by nine percentage points. For less-educated immigrants, LFPRs actually *rose* by over more than three points, to 92.5 percent over the same period of time. If a broad "demand-side" effect is really the dominant reason for the decline in LFPRs for this group, someone needs to explain why important subgroups of the cohort were not subject to it.

A fifth point is this: if demand-side effects were a truly significant determinant of changes in labor force participation patterns, one might expect that regional differentials would tend to diminish following such "shocks" as labor markets sought equilibrium. But nothing like this has occurred over the past several decades (see figure 7.5). Extreme variation characterized state-level prime-age male NILF levels in 2014, ranging from over 20 percent in West Virginia to 6 percent in Iowa. Moreover, some states with the highest inactivity levels were next to states with the lowest levels: West Virginia (20.3 percent) borders Maryland (8.7 percent), Maine (14.3 percent) borders New Hampshire (8.8 percent), New Mexico (17.4 percent) touches Utah (7.1 percent), and

FIGURE 7.4. LABOR FORCE PARTICIPATION RATES FOR NATIVE- AND FOREIGN-BORN PRIME-AGE MEN WITH LESS THAN A HIGH SCHOOL EDUCATION, 1994–2015

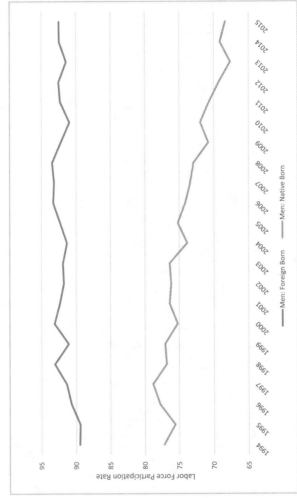

Notes: "nativity" is a variable that equals 1 if an individual was born either in a territory of the United States or born in one of the fifty United States; "nativity" equals 0 otherwise.

FIGURE 7.5: NON–LABOR FORCE RATES AMONG PRIME-AGE MALES BY STATE, 2015

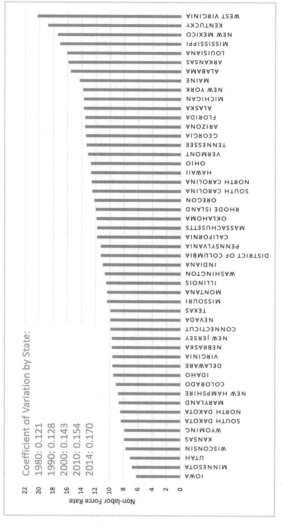

Coefficient of Variation by State:

1980: 0.121
1990: 0.128
2000: 0.143
2010: 0.154
2014: 0.170

Source: "CPS Table Creator," U.S. Census Bureau, retrieved on June 20, 2016, http://www.census.gov/cps/data/cpstablecreator.html.

so on. Moreover, these variations have increased over time. Growing long-term regional differences might be explained by institutional effects, as we shall soon see, or even supply-side effects. But this feature of contemporary U.S. labor markets is not easily explained in terms of demand-side effects.

Changes in demand for labor in general and less-skilled labor in particular have certainly played some role in the ominous work trends for U.S. men documented in this study. This is not a small matter of dispute. Specifically, the parallel trends in work-rate decline for prime-age U.S. men and women since roughly 2000 suggest that our relatively weak economic performance since then has reduced employment opportunities in contemporary America. But are such "demand" factors so distinctive and powerful to explain America's uniquely poor labor force participation trends for prime-age men since the 1960s? It would seem difficult to explain why this should be the case.

Of course, we should all welcome further research on the demand-driven aspect of the male work problem. But I would also suggest that supply-side factors (diminished incentive to work) and institutional factors (legal or other barriers to work) deserve closer examination than they have received in explaining the postwar collapse in male employment rates and the great male flight from work. I focus on these other two factors in the final two chapters.

CHAPTER 8

Dependence, Disability, and Living Standards for Un-Working Men

❧❧

How do America's un-working men support themselves? We can begin by looking at the Census Bureau's figures on household income for prime-age men by employment status (see figure 8.1). In 2014 (the most recent year available for such data), the CPS ASEC survey reported that the median earned income for prime-age men out of the labor force and not looking for work was zero. In other words, fully half of all NILFs reported no wage income at all. The average earned income for this group was barely $4,500. The median income for unemployed men came to $10,000, and their average income was about $22,000. The median income for men who had a job was $44,000 and their mean income was almost $57,000. When comparing average earnings for 2014 and 1965, adjusting for inflation, working men average considerably more income than two generations ago. Even currently unemployed men earn more. The earned income for NILFs, however, is lower now than two generations earlier.

FIGURE 8.1. MEAN INDIVIDUAL AND HOUSEHOLD WAGE INCOME FOR PRIME-AGE MEN 25–54 BY EMPLOYMENT STATUS (CPS ASEC SURVEY, 2014)

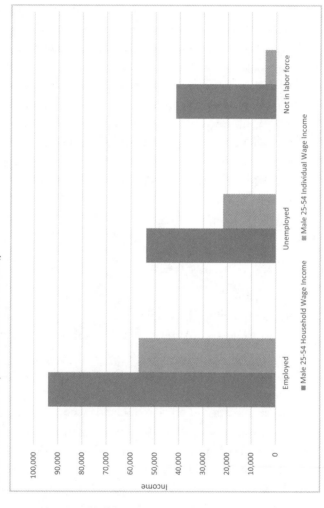

Source: "25–54 Individual Wage Income," CPS_tables, accessed July 27, 2016. Prince et al., July 2016.

While un-working prime-age men nowadays report practically no earned income of their own, they are not entirely without means. The prime-age male NILF household reported a median income of just under $25,000 and a mean income of more than $41,000. These totals were, of course, lower than for homes with working and unemployed prime-age men in them. Interestingly, however, the amount of additional household income available in homes with working, unemployed, and un-working men did not differ appreciably in 2014. In terms of mean income, the additional annual household resources beyond the prime-age male earned income were almost the same for un-working and working men ($37,000 vs. $38,000). The additional resources were actually greater in the NILF home than a home with an unemployed man ($37,000 vs. $32,000).

In sum, households with un-working prime-age men were poorer than homes with employed men, or, for that matter, unemployed men who were looking for work, and the differences in overall household income levels were almost entirely explained by the lack of earnings on the part of un-working men.

Sources of such additional household income differed substantially and in accordance with the employment status of a family's prime-age man. For men with jobs, the average spousal contribution was about $20,000—around twice as much as for unemployed men (about $11,000) and NILFs (under $10,000). A much higher fraction of working men had wives, two out of three, versus un-working men, two out of five. Wives contributed more in absolute terms to the household budget in homes with working men than in homes with un-working men, as well as a larger relative share of the remaining family income not accounted for by the man's earnings.

In addition to being supported by their spouses and other household members, the living expenses of un-working men today are subsidized by Uncle Sam. According to ASEC, the average amount of government benefits received by working prime-age men was just over $500 in 2014. For un-working prime-age men, the average was about $5,700, over ten times as much. Un-working prime-age men reportedly drew about two and a half times as much in the way of government support as their unemployed counterparts.

These ASEC numbers for government payments to un-working men, however, are underestimates—likely substantial ones. ASEC is notorious for understating the prevalence and amounts of transfer payments to recipients. It relies upon survey responses in its calculations for household income sources, and government benefits—especially means-tested "antipoverty" benefits—tend to be underreported. Even after Census Bureau statisticians' adjustments to compensate for such underreporting, ASEC figures for social benefits from many programs are far lower than the true sums administrative records report being allocated to recipients. A 2015 study on New York City, for example, found that the CPS headcount of beneficiaries missed "over one-third of housing assistance recipients, 40 percent of food stamp recipients and 60 percent of TANF and General Assistance recipients."[1] It also found that the dollar amounts of welfare transfers were dramatically underreported.[2]

A better source for information may be the already-mentioned SIPP, or the Survey for Income and Program Participation. As its name indicates, SIPP was designed specifically to measure "program participation." While there is evidence that it, too, underreports, researchers generally believe it comes closer to the mark than the CPS in estimating the true number of program enrollees and actual payments.

Table 8.1 presents results from an analysis of SIPP micro-data conducted by a research team supervised by Brigham Young University professor Joe Price. It shows patterns of reported government benefit payments for households with prime-age men in 2013, differentiated by employment status. It also offers corresponding figures from 1985 to give some sense of trends over time.

As can be seen, dependence upon "means-tested" benefits had become widespread by 2013. As of 2013, 27 percent of *all* prime-age men lived in homes receiving poverty-related benefits. The figure for 1985 was 11 percent. A full 23 percent of working prime-age men lived in homes that received means-tested benefits in 2013. But 63 percent of homes with un-working men reportedly received such assistance, 41 percent lived on food stamps (the Supplemental Nutritional Assistance Program), and 53 percent reported being on Medicaid. (Un-working men, incidentally, were routinely more dependent on such public assistance than those who were out of work but looking for a job.) In addition, such welfare dependence for NILFs seems to have shot up by nearly twenty percentage points since 1985. The increase

TABLE 8.1. DEMOGRAPHIC AND ECONOMIC CHARACTERISTICS OF HOUSEHOLDS ("CONSUMER UNITS") HEADED BY U.S. MEN 25–54 BY LABOR FORCE STATUS: CONSUMER EXPENDITURE SURVEY 2014 (INCOME, TAXES, AND EXPENDITURES IN CURRENT DOLLARS)

YEAR	EMPLOYMENT STATUS	ONE OR MORE MEANS TESTED BENEFITS	MEDICAID	TANF/AFDC	FOOD STAMPS (SNAP)	PROGRAM FOR WOMAN, INFANTS, AND CHILDREN (WIC)
1985	Total	11.1	7.0	2.0	5.9	1.7
	Employed	7.6	4.3	1.1	3.3	1.3
	Unemployed	36.3	26.2	12.4	33.3	6.1
	NILF	43.6	32.2	7.3	23.5	2.9
2013	Total	27.2	21.0	1.0	12.2	5.6
	Employed	23.6	18.0	0.7	9.2	5.5
	Unemployed	47.2	34.7	3.4	29.3	6.6
	NILF	63.0	52.5	3.8	41.4	5.4

Sources: Price et al. "sipp_table, unpartitioned sample," unpublished analysis, accessed on July 30, 2016; Survey of Income and Program Participation, U.S. Census Bureau accessed on August 3, 2016, http://www.census.gov/programs-surveys/sipp/data.html.

in NILF homes obtaining one or more means-tested benefits was much greater than homes with prime-age men who were unemployed but looking for work, never mind homes with working men in them—the only exceptions were for targeted benefit programs for children, such as WIC, insofar as un-working men were more likely to live in childless homes.

Means-tested benefits, of course, are not the only variety of government assistance that un-working men rely upon. Disability benefits—temporary or permanent pensions for those officially declared incapable of working to support themselves—are a major source of income for prime-age men who neither have a job nor are looking for one. By all indications, disability payments are an increasingly important source of support for such men.

Unfortunately, considerable uncertainty and even confusion exists about the true extent of NILF dependence upon U.S. disability programs. No central authority keeps track of America's many separate disability programs. The main program is Social Security Disability Insurance (SSDI). It dispensed more than $11 billion a month to over ten million beneficiaries as of late 2014.[3] There is also the Supplemental Security Insurance (SSI) program, which provided an additional $4.4 billion a month in late 2014 to some eight million claimants.[4] The Veterans Administration disability compensation program paid out another $4.5 billion a month to 3.5 million beneficiaries as of 2013.[5] On top of these and other less-familiar or well-tracked disability programs, there are also workers' compensation benefits at the state level.[6] The United States is currently spending hundreds of billions of dollars a year on disability payments and the bureaucracies that administer them. Yet we do not know exactly how much money is being devoted to such claims or how many people in America are receiving payouts from one or more of these programs.

Suffice it to say that researchers will seriously underestimate the scope and scale of disability payments in America today if they focus on SSDI alone. This, however, is exactly what the president's CEA seems to have done in its recent report on declining LFPRs for prime-age men in America:

> SSDI receipt rates have been rising among prime-age men for the last 50 years. Today, 3.3 percent of prime-age men receive SSDI payments. A number of research papers find that increases in the number of people receiving SSDI led to lower labor force participation among the general population . . . and to lower earnings . . . However, from 1967 until 2014, the percentage of prime-age men receiving disability insurance rose from 1 percent to 3 percent, not nearly enough to explain the 7.5-percentage-point decline in the labor force participation rate over that period . . . So while SSDI receipt's impact on prime-age male labor force participation is negative, under reasonable assumptions it is small and cannot

explain more than a portion of the overall decline in participation.[7]

The CEA's conclusion hinges on the assumption that SSDI is the only source of disability support available to un-workers today. But a more comprehensive assessment would recognize that un-workers can access disability funds from a multiplicity of programs that currently exist and that disability payments, like other of income sources, are fungible, meaning men can live on disability checks sent to others in their household.

Table 8.2 presents 2013 and 1985 SIPP data on disability program income for prime-age men, according to employment status. Over these three decades, the share of prime-age men reporting disability payments rose from 4.2 percent to 6.3 percent. Only about 2 percent of working men claimed such benefits in both years. For unemployed prime-age men, the share was about 4 percent in 2013, a very slight decline over the intervening generation. But an explosion of disability recipiency was registered for NILFs. This group accounted for most of the nationwide increase in prime-age disability payments. By 2013, 57 percent of prime-age un-working men lived in homes reporting disability benefits, nearly twenty percentage points higher than it had been in 1985 and twice as high as the CEA assessment of the NILF problem indicated. If we look at NILF households rather than simply at the un-working men in them, we see that the incidence of disability benefit recipiency is even higher: nearly two-thirds

(66 percent) of those homes reported taking in money from at least one government disability program in 2013. Roughly a quarter of the prime-age NILF men with disability benefits reported receiving such benefits from two or more programs.

TABLE 8.2. REPORTED RECIPIENCE OF DISABILITY BENEFITS FOR PRIME-AGE MEN 25–54 AND THEIR HOUSEHOLDS, SIPP SURVEY, 1985 AND 2013 (PERCENT)

Year	Employment Status	Prime-Age Male Disability Benefit	Two or More Prime-Age Male Disability Benefits	Disability Benefit, Household Level	Two Disability Benefits, Household Level
1985	Total	4.2	0.6	13.1	1.9
1985	Employed	2.0	0.04	10.1	1.1
1985	Unemployed	4.7	0.17	23.7	2.2
1985	NILF	38.3	9.9	51.9	13.6
2013	Total	6.3	1.1	14.9	2.4
2013	Employed	2.5	0.1	10.6	1.4
2013	Unemployed	4.3	—	21.6	2.2
2013	NILF	56.5	14.1	66.0	15.4

Sources: Price et al., "SIPP table, unpartitioned sample," unpublished analysis, retrieved on July 30, 2016; "Survey of Income and Program Participation," U.S. Census Bureau, http://www.census.gov/programs-surveys/sipp/data.html. Retrieved on August 3, 2016.

A small group reported benefits from three or more programs. By 2013, nearly one in six (15 percent) of NILF homes were reportedly taking home benefits from two or more such programs. And, as previously noted, SIPP members are somewhat likely to understate the true extent of dependence upon government social benefits.

Table 8.2 is only a first step toward determining the actual role that disability programs—and the means-tested benefit programs that disability eligibility facilitates—play in financing the living standards of the ever-growing cadre of prime-age men who have retreated out of the workforce. We could gain a better look through the use of "linked administrative data," the strategy pursued in the aforementioned study of welfare benefit recipiency in New York City. This work is beyond the scope of just this study, however. I am hopeful that researchers in the U.S. government, the academy, and policy think tanks will soon take up this challenge. For now, however, it is only possible to simply observe that the role of disability programs in supporting NILF households is clearly much greater than many leading economists and policy experts believe.

I have already pointed out the counterintuitive increase over time in state-level disparities in prime-age male LFPRs in chapter 7. Growing disability and welfare dependence on the part of the NILF population may help to explain this paradox. As the Ethics and Public Policy Center's Henry Olsen has argued, existing social welfare programs have the perverse and unintended effect of binding recipients to the locality in which they draw benefits—whether there are more promising economic opportunities elsewhere or not. Growing disability and welfare dependence may thereby be contributing to the malfunction of the national labor market in matching the un-working with work.

If social welfare and disability programs in effect tether recipients to the localities and states where benefits are dispensed, we might expect state-level disparities in prime-age male LFPRs to track relatively weakly with state-level differences in public program benefit levels—but also to see meaningful correlations between work patterns and social welfare benefit packages at the state level for immigrants to America, since the move from overseas to the United States in effect provides a "natural experiment" through which to observe the impact of the U.S. welfare state on work incentives. Sure enough, there is no meaningful correlation between implicit state-level benefit packages (as calculated by Michael Tanner and Charles Hughes of the Cato Institute) and prime-age male state-level LFPRs: but at the same time, we can detect a meaningful correspondence between levels of welfare/disability benefits on the one hand and immigrants' welfare dependence and labor force behavior on the other.[8] Consider the test case of prime-age male Latino immigrants in Texas and California. California has a generous and expansive set of state-level social guarantees; Texas does not. California makes it easy for immigrants to obtain social welfare benefits;

Texas does not. By Tanner's calculations, the implicit welfare benefit package for a family of four could be equivalent to up to a $17-an-hour wage in California for 2013—as opposed to $6-an-hour wage in Texas (a level then below the national minimum wage). Sure enough: as figure 8.2 demonstrates, in 2014 prime-age male LFPRs for Hispanic immigrants were lower in California than in Texas, as were work rates—this, for one of America's hardest working demographic groups. Utilization of means-tested welfare benefits was also evidently much higher for immigrant Latinos in California than for those in Texas, according to the CPS data. The negative supply-side effects on work exerted by our welfare/disability state are evidently operative—but the complex nature of that system's variegated and byzantine rules makes this more difficult to discern than might reasonably be expected, at least at first glance.[9]

We have examined income and its sources for the prime-age un-working man, but still need to get a sense of his living standard. Income levels are a highly unreliable predictor of consumption levels for the poor and near poor, as I have demonstrated elsewhere.[10] To assess consumption levels, it's better to look at expenditure patterns, which we can attempt

Notes: "nativity" is a variable defined by citizenship status—native born (born in the United States or born to native parents abroad) or foreign born (born abroad to foreign parents or currently not a citizen). Sample size—without population weights: California (71), Texas (25); with population weights: California (129,312), Texas (51,857).

Source: "Current Population Survey, Annual Social and Economic Supplement (ASEC) 2015," U.S. Census Bureau, retrieved July 28, 2016.

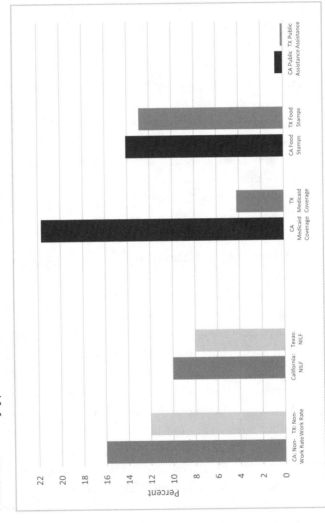

FIGURE 8.2. EMPLOYMENT STATUS AND MEANS-TESTED WELFARE BENEFIT RECIPIENCE: PRIME-AGE MALE 25–54 HISPANIC IMMIGRANTS, CALIFORNIA VS. TEXAS, 2014

to divine from the Bureau of Labor Statistics Consumer Expenditure Survey (CEX), annually conducted since the early 1980s. For some reason, CEX bundles unemployment and NILF men together in the same category. As we have seen, NILF prime-age men outnumber unemployed men by roughly three to one. These days, the "nonworking" men in this category overwhelmingly comprise NILFs.

According to the CEX, average 2014 income for prime-age male homes with a working man was three times higher than those with an unemployed/NILF man: $90,000 vs. $29,000 (see table 8.3). Homes with prime-age male workers contributed about $13,000 in personal taxes to the government; homes with nonworkers only contributed about $1,000. As for expenditures, unemployed/NILF homes in 2014 had about $31,000 in reported spending powers, and homes with a working man had about $62,000, twice as much. Unemployed/NILF homes also reported more expenditures than after-tax income, suggesting no savings or wealth building.

Yet, while homes with nonworking prime-age males generally had a lower living standard than homes with prime-age men with paying jobs, these households were by no means at the bottom of either the U.S. income or consumption spectrums. In 2014, the average income for a prime-age male home with a nonworking man (unemployed or not in labor force) would have placed it in the fourth income decile. Its spending power also would have placed it in the fourth decile of the U.S. consumption stratum.[11] Ironically, that's roughly where the notional "working class" was situated in

TABLE 8.3. DEMOGRAPHIC AND ECONOMIC CHARACTERISTICS OF HOUSEHOLDS ("CONSUMER UNITS") HEADED BY U.S. MEN 25–54 BY LABOR FORCE STATUS: CONSUMER EXPENDITURE SURVEY, 2014 (INCOME, TAXES, AND EXPENDITURES IN CURRENT DOLLARS)

	TOTAL	EMPLOYED OR SELF-EMPLOYED	UNEMPLOYED OR NILF
Median Age	40	40	44
Percentage Married	58	59	37
Mean Persons per Consumer Unit	2.8	2.9	2.6
Mean Earners per Consumer Unit	1.6	1.7	0.5
Mean Number of Vehicles	1.9	2.0	1.2
Percent with at Least One Vehicle	88	90	65
Percent Homeowners	57	59	37
Total Consumer Unit Income before Taxes	84,897	89,545	29,483
Earned Income	76,038	81,149	16,161
Total Consumer Unit Personal Taxes	12,019	12,951	1,009
Total Consumer Unit Expenditures	59,488	61,784	31,310

Note: Retired men 25–54 excluded from this table.

Source: "1996/2014 Bureau of Labor Statistics Consumer Expenditure Survey: Males between 25 and 54," Bureau of Labor Statistics. Provided by Price et al. Retrieved on August 2, 2016.

days of yore.

Although a considerable fraction of NILF households may fall below the federal poverty threshold, the important fact here may be that roughly two-thirds of households were not below the official poverty line. Further, the CEX data suggests that "consumption poverty"—as opposed to officially measured "income poverty"—affected a distinctly smaller share of households containing prime-age men who were not at work. In table 8.3, expenditures for prime-age male unemployed/NILF homes in 2014 averaged roughly twice the official poverty line for households with that number of members.[12] Recall that the nonworking men in table 8.3 also received nonmonetized benefits from the government that were not included in the spending reckoning, subsidies that made their living standard higher in relation to the national average. No less important, the living standard of nonworking households appears to have risen in recent years. If we control for price changes and household size, per capita spending power was about 14 percent higher for prime-age male nonworking homes in 2014 than in 1996.[13]

Households with nonworking prime-age men are hardly rich, but they are by no means as poor as some might assume. In 2014, their average reported household expenditures were about two-fifths lower than the average for the country as a whole—but they were also about a third higher than the average for the bottom income quintile.[14] In 2014, over 60 percent of households in the bottom quintile of the CEX were female headed (typically, single-mother homes). All in all, nonworking men—and by extension, the great majority of nonworking men who were not looking for work—appear to be better off than tens of millions of other Americans today, including the millions of single mothers who are either working or seeking work.

How do prime-age NILFs support themselves? The short answer is, apparently they don't. Relatives and friends and the U.S. government float these long-term nonparticipants in the workforce, most of whom, as seen in chapter 6, are doing little to improve themselves or their chances for employment. And many un-working men have a surprisingly high living standard, given their apparent lack of earned income. (Note that we have no information on the fraction of these NILFs who are in reality working at least part-time off the books or under the table. This is a gap that should, at the very least, not go unmentioned here.)

Whatever else the tables and figures in this chapter may indicate, they have underscored an almost revolutionary change in male attitudes toward work and dependence in postwar America. It is impossible to imagine any earlier generation in which such a huge swath of prime-age men would voluntarily absent themselves from the workforce, living instead on the largesse of women they knew and tax-payers they did not. It is impossible to imagine any earlier generation of younger American men reconciling themselves in such tremendous numbers to a daily routine of idleness, financed substantially by some government programs that certified them as incapable of working. And it is likewise impossible to imagine that any earlier generation of working and taxpaying Americans would find acceptable our nation's current arrangements for supporting men who are neither working nor looking for work.

CHAPTER 9

Criminality and the Decline of Work
for American Men

≥≤

AMERICA'S GREAT male flight from work began in earnest around 1965 and has continued virtually without pause since then. The timing of this fateful shift in work patterns may be significant. The year marked a watershed moment in American social history. It was then President Johnson rolled out his "Great Society" programs, giving birth to the modern welfare state as we know it today. The Immigration and Nationality Act of 1965 initiated a huge new wave of immigration into the United States, substantially increasing legal and illegal immigration, boosting the country's population, and altering its ethnic composition over the past half century.

But 1965 was also an important social milestone for another reason: it was roughly then that a national crime wave began to sweep over the United States. The reaction to the explosion of criminality crystallized in a national consensus that America should suppress crime by arresting, convicting, and incarcerating felons. For more than a generation,

U.S. incarceration rates have been unique among advanced democracies. Released felons and ex-prisoners form a far larger fraction of the working-age male population than any other population group. These men with criminal records are disproportionately people of color and/or those with low educational attainment. Amazingly, however, the U.S. government does not today bother to collect tinformation on their employment patterns.

As we shall see, a single variable—having a criminal record—is a key missing piece in explaining why work rates and LFPRs have collapsed much more dramatically in America than other affluent Western societies over the past two generations. This single variable also helps explain why the collapse has been so much greater for American men than women and why it has been so much more dramatic for African American men and men with low educational attainment than for other prime-age men in the United States.

Some background here. Although crime statistics in America were arguably primitive half a century ago, such data as were available suggested crime levels had been more or less stable over the postwar era. Public perception also essentially tracked with those crime statistics. Starting in the mid-1960s, though, crime skyrocketed, and popular perceptions about crime followed. Public safety was generally believed to be worsening, perhaps dramatically. In the 1970s, Americans responded by enacting and enforcing more stringent measures against crime at the federal, state, and local levels.

Vastly more convicts were sent to prison, and even more felons were processed through the criminal system via probation and "community supervision."

After two decades, reported U.S. crime rates for all major types of crime finally declined (see figure 9.1). Crime rates in America today are thought to be more or less back to levels of the early 1960s. Incarceration rates, on the other hand, are roughly five times as high today as they were in the late 1960s.

The correspondence between crime and punishment is not our concern here. Rather, it is the impact of the upsurge in arrests, felony convictions, and incarcerations on the labor market. To understand the impact of this enormous social change on male work patterns in modern America, one must first attempt to estimate the number of men caught up in our criminal justice system over the past several decades, as well as the demographic and social characteristics of these men. Then one must attempt to assess the impact on postwar America's changing employment trends for men according to age, social characteristics, and criminal history.

As a direct consequence of crime and punishment trends since the 1960s, American society now contains a truly vast, if generally invisible, army of noninstitutionalized felons and ex-prisoners. These are overwhelmingly adult men convicted of serious criminal offenses who have been punished with prison time or probation, but who are now part of our general population.

FIGURE 9.1. U.S. Crime and Imprisonment Rates, 1960–2010

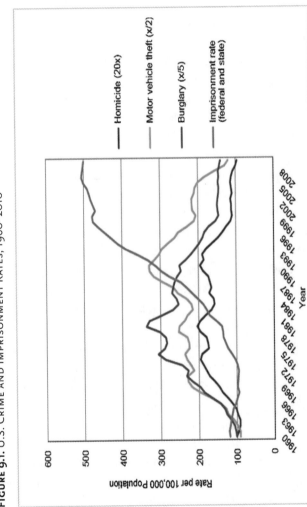

Note: The different crime rates have been rescaled, as noted in the figure, to facilitate comparison of time trends.

Most well-informed readers know that the number of U.S. convicts behind bars has soared in America in recent decades and that the United States currently has a higher share of its populace in jail or prison than almost any other country. But only a tiny fraction of all Americans ever convicted of a felony are actually incarcerated at this moment. Maybe 90 percent of all sentenced felons today are out of confinement and living more or less among us.

How can this be? It comes down to the basic arithmetic of sentencing and incarceration.

First, very few convicted felons are sent away for life. According to the Justice Department's Bureau of Justice Statistics, average time served in state penitentiaries for an imprisoned first offender in recent years is just over two years.[1] More than six hundred thousand convicts are released from prison every year,[2] and many do not return. In addition, many convicted felons are never confined in the first place. They instead undergo "community supervision," such as probation. In 2006 (the most recent year for which the Bureau of Justice Statistics publishes such figures), nearly a third of the 1.1 million felons convicted in state courts were sentenced neither to prison nor jail, but instead placed directly under some form of extramural supervision.[3] Thus, correctional release and sentenced community supervision guarantee a steady annual "flow" of convicted felons joining the considerable "stock" of felons and ex-felons already on the street. Amazingly, there seem to be no official estimates for either

America's ex-prisoner population or its unimprisoned felon and ex-felon population. Some researchers, however, have attempted to approximate the dimensions of this invisible population, and their findings are staggering. For 2004, one demographic reconstruction put the population of America's current felons and ex-felons at more than 16 million.[4] A subsequent, still unpublished study estimated that the cohort of current and former felons in America had reached nearly 20 million by the year 2010—four times larger, the researchers estimated, than 30 years earlier. They also estimated that slightly over 5 million of these at-large felons were released former convicts (see figure 9.2).

These two studies approximated the civilian noninstitutional ex-prisoner and felon population by sex. Unsurprisingly, the overwhelming majority of this population were men. An estimated 4.7 million adult men were at-large ex-prisoners as of 2010. The estimate of adult men who had been convicted of any felony came to over 14 million of the nearly 20 million current and former felons in 2010 who were adult men no longer behind bars. Their estimates indicate that approximately 12 percent of all civilian noninstitutional adult males in 2010 had a felony conviction in their background. Since the incarceration explosion is a relatively recent phenomenon, this also means that the proportion of prime-age men with a felony conviction was appreciably higher than 12 percent and the proportion for African American men higher still.

FIGURE 9.2. ESTIMATED POPULATION OF FELONS AND EX-FELONS: UNITED STATES, 1948–2010

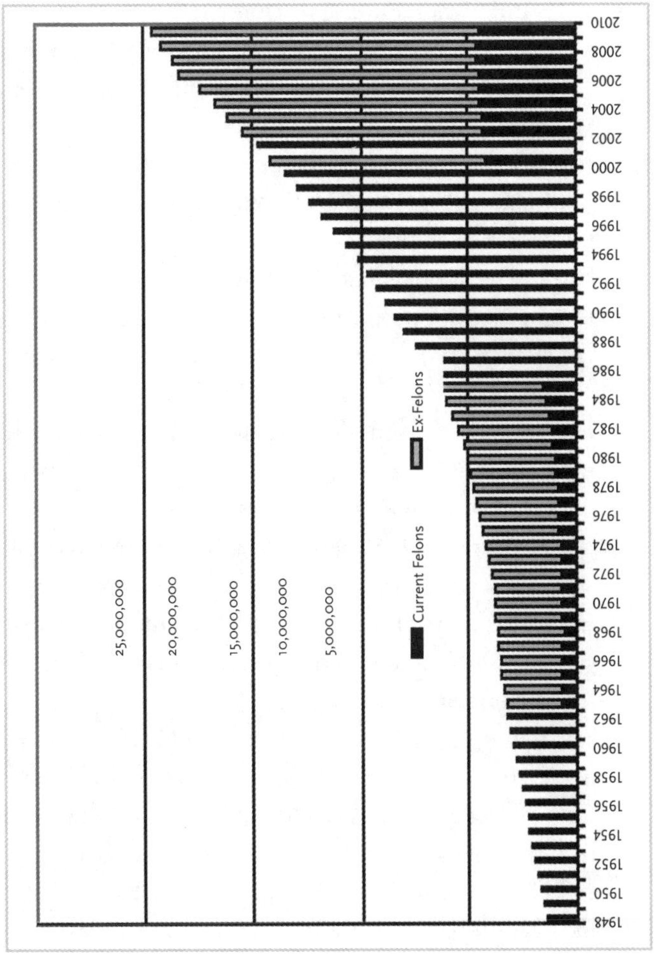

Source: Sarah Shannon et al., "The Growth, Scope, and Spatial Distribution of America's Criminal Class, 1948–2010," unpublished paper, 2015, retrieved on August 2, 2016.

If America's felon population continued to grow at the same pace as the 2004–10 period, we would expect that total to surpass 23 million persons by the end of 2016 at the latest. America's population of noninstitutionalized adults with a felony conviction somewhere in their past will almost certainly exceed 20 million by the end of 2016—and the current total for men within this group could now exceed 17 million, or 13 percent of all male adults in America. Needless to say, this means the proportion of prime-age men with felony convictions in the general population has been rising, too.

These estimates reveal some relationship between the adult felon population and prime-age male LFPRs at the state level in the census years 1980, 1990, 2000, and 2010 (see figure 9.3). Data and methodological issues attend this comparison, but there does seem to be a fairly modest correlation between state-level felon population and state-level prime-age male LFPRs (r-square of 0.24). Yet such high altitude comparisons cannot substitute for actual examination of individuals and their characteristics.[5]

Now, let us consider estimates of the likelihood of criminal justice system history—arrest, felony conviction, incarceration—for adult men by demographic and social characteristics over the postwar decades. Sadly, the most recent study by U.S. government researchers on the lifetime likelihood of incarceration was published in 2003 and ends at the year 2001.[6] The circumstances of this ex-prisoner and at-large felon population are, it seems, a matter of almost complete

FIGURE 9.3. PERCENTAGE OF PRIME-AGE MEN (25–54) NOT IN THE LABOR FORCE VS. THE PERCENTAGE OF MEN AND WOMEN WITH A FELONY CONVICTION, BY DECADE: 1980, 1990, 2000, AND 2010

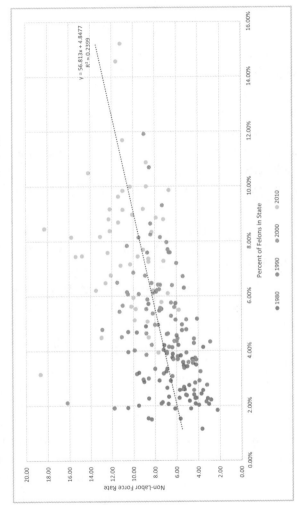

Source: Sarah Flood et al., *Integrated Public Use Microdata Series, Current Population Survey: Version 4.0* (Minneapolis: University of Minnesota, 2015); Sarah Shannon et. al., "The Growth, Scope, and Spatial Distribution of Class 1948–2010," unpublished paper, retrieved on August 2, 2016.

indifference to the rest of us. These people only show up in our national statistics if and when they again run afoul of the criminal justice system.[7]

Some scholars have attempted to reconstruct those trends themselves. One study by Harvard's Bruce Western and Becky Pettit of the University of Texas estimated the risk of incarceration up to age thirty-five for young men of different ethnicities and educational levels (see figure 9.4). They concluded that the risk of incarceration varied wildly according to ethnicity and education. For non-Hispanic white men with twelve years of education, for example, the odds of incarceration by age thirty-five were about 5 percent for those born between 1957 and 1964. On the other hand, the odds were about 18 percent for non-Hispanic whites with less than a high school education. For a non-Hispanic black man with a high school education, the odds were over 25 percent. The odds were 58 percent for a black high school dropout. For Latinos with less than twelve years of education, the odds were about 23 percent: higher than for similar whites, but much lower than for similar blacks.

Western and Pettit also calculated that the risk of imprisonment for men ages thirty to thirty-four rose sharply between 1979 and 2009, going up for every subgroup, irrespective of ethnicity or education. But in absolute terms, the risks went up much more for non-Hispanic blacks than for non-Hispanic whites or Latinos and much more for men with less than a high school education than for any others. Between

FIGURE 9.4. CUMULATIVE RISK OF INCARCERATION RATE BY RACE AND EDUCATIONAL ATTAINMENT, MEN 21–35

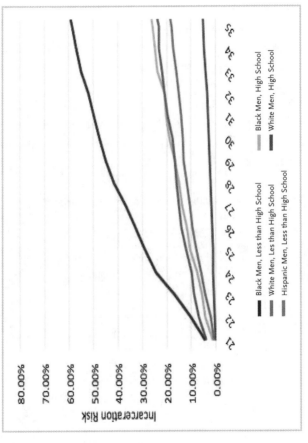

Source: "Technical Report on REVISED Population Estimates and NLSY79 Analysis Tables for the Pew Public Safety and Mobility Project," Western and Pettit. July 2, 2009. (Accessed July 29, 2016.

1979 and 2009, they found that the risk of imprisonment rose from 1.4 percent to 5.4 percent for all white men in their early thirties and from 3.8 percent to 28 percent for those without a high school diploma or GED. For all black men, the corresponding numbers were 10.4 percent and 26.8 percent—and for those without a high school degree, 14.7 percent and 68 percent (see table 9.1).

Now I turn to male employment patterns by criminal justice history. Because the U.S. government publishes no data on this topic, contemporary economists have almost entirely avoided it as a research issue.[8] Thus, what I present in figures

TABLE 9.1. ESTIMATED PROBABILITY OF AT LEAST ONE INCARCERATION BY RACE AND EDUCATIONAL ATTAINMENT: U.S. MALES 30–34, 1979 VS. 2009

		LESS THAN HIGH SCHOOL	HIGH SCHOOL/ GED	SOME COLLEGE	ALL
1979	White	3.8	1.5	0.4	1.4
	Black	14.7	11.0	5.3	10.4
	Hispanic	4.1	2.9	1.1	2.8
2009	White	28.0	6.2	1.2	5.4
	Black	68.0	21.4	6.6	26.8
	Hispanic	19.6	9.2	3.4	12.2

Sources: Bruce Western and Becky Pettit, "Technical Report on Revised Population Estimates and NLSY79 Analysis Tables for the Pew Public Safety and Mobility Project," accessed on July 29, 2016.

9.5 and 9.6 is a peek at the relationship between employment and criminal history for prime-age men in modern America as afforded by the National Longitudinal Survey of Youth (NLSY; see figs. 9.5 and 9.6).[9]

The NLSY is (to my knowledge) one of only two large-scale surveys in America today that asks respondents about their antisocial behavior and criminal justice system history, along with the more conventional battery of social and economic questions.[10] A team led by Professor Joe Price of Brigham Young University prepared these figures at my request for this study.

Data from the NLSY on employment history are not easily harmonized with the Bureau of Labor Statistics own taxonomy for employment status (working/unemployed/out of workforce). For one thing, respondents do not always report their entire work history for the year in question or whether they were looking for work when they did not have a job. In figures 9.5 and 9.6, I categorize as "NILF" those men who reported having no work for all weeks reported, irrespective of whether they were seeking work. I categorize as "unemployed" those men who reported spending less than 40 percent of the year employed. Those who reported spending more than 40 percent of the year at work are categorized as being employed. Therefore, these data are not directly comparable with corresponding Bureau of Labor Statistics data on work rates or inactivity rates by age, ethnicity, and education. Even so, the patterns they reveal are highly informative.

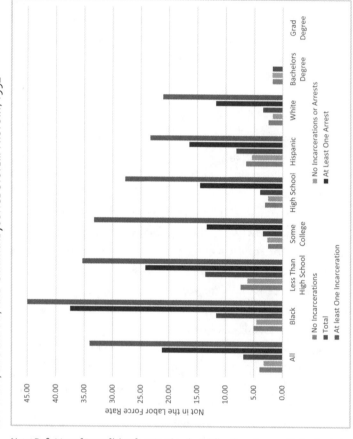

Figure 9.5. Percent of U.S. Men 30–34 out of the Labor Force, by Ethnicity, Education, and Criminal Justice System History, 1992

Note: Definition of "out of labor force" in this chart differs from Bureau of Labor Statistics definition. See text for discussion.

Source: Felony conviction rates: "Table 4.5- Percent of Men Out of the Labor Force Using the LFSY79," Price et al., unpublished tables, retrieved on July 29, 2016.

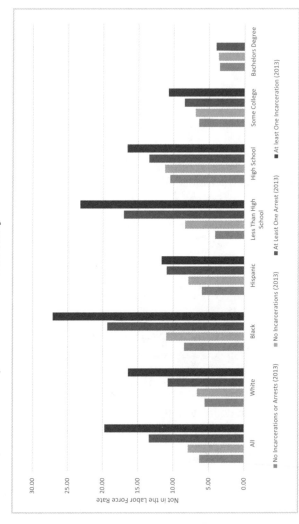

Figure 9.6. Percent of U.S. Men 30–34 out of the Labor Force, by Ethnicity, Education, and Criminal Justice System History, 2013

Note: Definition of "out of labor force" in this chart differs from Bureau of Labor Statistics definition. See text for discussion.

NLSY data permit analysis of employment patterns by age, ethnicity, education, and criminal justice system history in the years 1992 (for NLSY79 men between the ages of twenty-five and thirty-four), 2012 (for NLSY men between the ages of forty-five and fifty-four), and 2013 (for NLSY97 men between the ages of thirty and thirty-four). For every year under consideration, for every prime-age male group, for every ethnicity, and for every educational background, there is a robust and unmistakable labor market hierarchy with respect to criminal history.

Men with at least one spell in prison always have the lowest employment rates and the highest rates of absence from the workforce. Next come men who have at least one arrest in their past. The highest work rates and the lowest levels of absence from the labor market are those who have no incarceration history or no history of either arrest or incarceration (usually the group with the very highest labor market involvement). While NLSY does not have information on felony convictions per se from NLSY (i.e., for persons sentenced for a serious crime but including those who did not serve time in prison) we would expect work rates for the overall felon population to fall between those of ex-prisoners and those of men who had been arrested at least once but never went to prison.

In 2012–13, using my own employment status categories, a man thirty–to–thirty-four years of age who was arrested at least once was twice as likely to be out of the labor force as one never arrested or incarcerated (13.4 percent vs. 6.4 percent). A man who had been to prison was three times as likely to be out of the workforce (19.7 percent vs. 6.4 percent). Men forty-five–to–fifty-four with at least one arrest were twice as likely as those who had no arrests or incarcerations to be out of the workforce (27.1 percent vs. 12.8 percent), and those with a prison history were three times as likely (39.1 percent vs. 12.8 percent).

In 2012–13, the odds of being out of the labor force were three times higher for those who spent time in prison than those never arrested or imprisoned among men thirty to thirty-four for blacks and whites alike. Among those forty-five–to–fifty-four, the odds of being out of the workforce were over 40 percent for black men, two times the odds for their counterparts with no criminal justice history. The odds were 35 percent for white males—more than four times the odds for their white counterparts with no history in the criminal justice system.

Also noteworthy is the impact of educational attainment. While absence from the workforce of course was more likely for men with lower levels of education, workforce presence varied tremendously within each educational grouping according to criminal history. Among those forty-five–to–fifty-four, for example, a high school graduate with no criminal history had about a one in seven chance of being out of the workforce; the odds for one with a history of prison time were about one in three. For men thirty to thirty-four, a man with no high school degree but also no incarceration was less likely to be out of the workforce than his counterparts with high school degrees—or even some college—and at least one arrest.

Perhaps most critically, the workforce absence rates for *less-educated* young men varied dramatically by criminal history. Among less-educated young men who had already been to prison, nearly one in four were out of the labor force. For those with at least one arrest, over one in six were out of the labor force. For those with no arrest or prison record, fewer than one in twenty were out of the labor force. And these 2013 results were not a "one off." Two decades earlier, the original cohort of NLSY men, then ages twenty-five to thirty-four, offered similar findings.

Without recounting the results for work-rate patterns for prime-age men, we can simply note that these too are strongly influenced by criminal history, irrespective of year, age, ethnicity, or education.

The preliminary and exploratory findings in figures 9.5 and 9.6, which are of limited comparability with official U.S. employment data, nevertheless make a telling point: criminal justice history looks to be a key variable in the collapse of work and the flight from work for U.S. men over the postwar era. To date, however, this has been what statisticians call an "omitted variable"—an unrecognized factor with a powerful independent influence whose omission biases any assessment of other examined factors—in most analyses of the American male work problem. Lacking easy access to such data, most analyses have focused on things that are easier to observe statistically—somewhat like the proverbial drunk searching for his car keys under the streetlight, regardless of whether those keys are actually lying under the light or not.

Putting criminal history into the picture helps answer a number of otherwise puzzling questions. It helps explain why U.S. prime-age male LFPR trends look so dismal in relation to other affluent OECD countries. No other OECD country has anything like our share of working-age men with prison or conviction records. It also helps to explain the extraordinary slide in work rates and LFPRs among the less-educated prime-age men group, in which arrests, felony convictions, and prison sentences have been most heavily concentrated. And it helps to explain the remarkable gap in LFPRs between low-skilled prime-age immigrant men and low-skilled native-born men (who are far more likely to have criminal records in America).

Much further work will be needed to come up with reasonable quantitative estimates of the impact of criminal history in depressing work rates and LFPRs. By the same token, the paths or mechanisms by which criminal history affects labor market performance need to be examined much more carefully and understood much better than they are today.[11] We do not know what fraction of our growing corps of un-working prime-age men have a criminal record—or what fraction of those who have a criminal record are getting by, after a fashion, by claiming means-tested benefits or disability stipends themselves or drawing upon such benefits awarded to others. We should want to know just such things, and more, about the collision between the flight from work, criminality, and dependence.

It's important, however, not to overemphasize the role of criminality in the decline of male work over the postwar period. It is just one factor, an important and typically overlooked factor, but still just one factor. We should also remember that the great male flight from work had already been under way for more than a decade and a half before the U.S. male population of ex-prisoners and at-large felons began to soar in the early 1980s and that, curiously enough, the explosive growth of that "criminal class" after 1980 seemingly did little or nothing to speed the pace of decline for prime-age male LFPRs over the following three-plus decades.

At the end of the day, I believe that appreciating that our growing new class of men without work looks to be disproportionately composed of people with a tangled history of criminal justice system encounters will put us on a better path to dealing with their work problems, which also happen to be ours.

CHAPTER 10

What Is to Be Done?

THE DEATH of work for a large and ever-growing contingent of America's manhood is a peculiar and historically unprecedented problem. It's so very foreign to our previous way of life that we have yet to put a name to it. Yet this mass voluntary flight from work by men—this hitherto nameless problem—lies at the center of so much of America's new dysfunction and despair. It could hardly be otherwise. A Depression-scale collapse in employment for men, which is what we are witnessing today, could hardly help but have far-reaching and highly destructive reverberations, regardless of why these workless men no longer hold down jobs.

Imagine how different our country would be if another 9 to 10 million American men—most of them of prime working age—held down paying jobs today. That is the difference between the male work rates America enjoyed in 1965 and those now. (And yes, of course, it would also be beneficial to make up the "jobs deficit" that women have suffered since the beginning of the twenty-first century, though it is on a very different scale.) The collapse of work for the U.S. male, effected by a huge flight from work by grown men, is the elephant in our public square. It is a problem so urgent, so immense that it should demand immediate attention and action, though it is one we have somehow collectively managed more or less to ignore (a few honorable exceptions noted). I hope this study can help bring our "men without work" problem into focus so that Americans across the political spectrum can fathom the seriousness of this situation and begin to think about the ways that we, as a country, can address it.

Reasonable and well-informed people will disagree about the factors responsible for the great male flight from work in postwar America. They will also argue over the relative importance of some causes in relation to others. I believe, however, that there will be little disagreement in any quarter about the consequences of this strange new problem for our nation.

Economically, declining LFPRs and falling work rates have made for slower economic growth, widening gaps in income and wealth, greater budgetary pressures, and higher deficits and national debt. They have likewise increased the risk of poverty in the United States, not least for the children whose fathers are found in our huge army of men without work.

Socially, the male retreat from the labor force has further exacerbated family breakdown, promoted welfare dependence, recast "disability" into a viable alternative lifestyle, and routinized the support of men of prime working age by women. In addition, it has directly undermined prospects for social mobility. Americans may be the hardest working people of any affluent society in the world today, yet no other developed nation simultaneously floats such a large proportion of its prime-age men entirely outside the labor force— neither working, nor looking for work, nor doing much of anything else. Whatever the reasons or the motivations, they are essentially living off the rest of us. Social cohesion is a direct casualty of this development, and social trust could scarcely help but be degraded by it as well.

Politically, this death of work seems largely to have meant the death of civic engagement, community participation, and voluntary association for un-working men, too. Thus, we witness a still-growing phenomenon of American men in the prime of life who are not only disengaged from civil society, but also who require that same civil society's indefinite largesse to pay their way through life. This state of affairs may not quite be the "custodial democracy" my colleague Charles Murray warned of a generation ago, but it is uncomfortably close to it nonetheless.[1]

The death of work has ushered in additional costs at the personal and social levels that may be difficult to quantify but are easy to describe. These include the corrosive effects of prolonged idleness on personality and behavior, the loss of self-esteem and the respect of others that may attend a man's voluntary loss of economic independence, and the loss of meaning and fulfillment that work demonstrably brings to so many (though admittedly not all) people. Thus, the great male flight from work may well have increased our nation's burden of misery in an incalculable but nonetheless immediate manner. Should this come as a surprise? Hardly. The surprise would be if a social emasculation on this scale had increased the *happiness* of those concerned.

It is high time for American citizens and policymakers to recognize the American male's postwar flight from work for what it is: a grave social ill. It is imperative for the future health of our nation that we make a determined and sustained commitment to bringing these detached men back— back into the workplace, back into their families, back into our civil society.

I do not propose here to offer a comprehensive program to accomplish this great goal. This is not a "how to" book. America's "men without work" problem is immense and complex and has been gathering fully for two generations. Reversing it will surely require action on many different fronts—and certainly not just governmental action. It will also require suggestions and strategies from voices across the political spectrum; only a broad and inclusive approach will develop and sustain the consensus needed to turn this tide.

In the spirit of kicking off just such a discussion and debate, I can begin by suggesting we devote closer attention to three broad issues: (1) revitalizing American business and its job-generating capacities, (2) reducing the immense and perverse disincentives against male work embedded in our social welfare programs, and (3) coming to terms with the enormous challenge of bringing convicts and felons back into our economy and society.

Of the American economy's current ailments, the declining dynamism of U.S. businesses is among the most worrisome. Economists Ian Hathaway and Robert E. Litan have traced a long-term decline in business formation in the United States.[2] More U.S. businesses have closed than opened in each year since the 2008 crash. According to Hathaway and Litan, "Business deaths now exceed business births for the first time in the thirty-plus-year history of our data."[3] Furthermore, the decline in business creation is not limited to certain regions, but instead appears to be a nationwide trend. Not surprisingly, a loss of what Raven Molloy of the Federal Reserve and her colleagues term "labor market fluidity" has accompanied this decline in business dynamism.[4] They demonstrate that this loss in labor market fluidity has taken place over the years covered by the Hathaway-Litan study. Many forces may be at play here. Suffice it say that entrepreneurship is crucial to job creation and that America's growing regulatory burden is not the recipe for encouraging entrepreneurship. As the Hudson Institute's Marie-Joseé Kravis has observed, "Almost three decades of slower churn in the flow of business formation and business deaths, of less-dynamic labor markets, and of flat income growth point urgently to the need for better policy."[5]

As for social welfare policy, we have seen the insidious role that disability programs play in sustaining the no-work lifestyle for grown men. Disability insurance has an indispensable role to play for those who truly cannot support themselves and others due to impairment. But across the entire public policy research community, regardless of partisan preferences, there is widespread agreement that U.S. disability programs today are subject to widespread abuse and "gaming." The disability rolls should not constitute a holding pen for men who cannot find work or do not want it. It is time for a thorough reform of these programs and a shift away from an approach that rewards helplessness to one that emphasizes personal responsibility. If a "work first" principle informed our social welfare policies, we would be emphasizing training and education, job placement, tax credits—performance-conditioned benefits—instead of pensioning men off into permanent retirement in the prime of their lives at taxpayer expense. Twenty years ago—after a national consensus on the moral hazard of publicly subsidizing unwed motherhood finally crystallized—the United States enacted a largely successful "welfare reform" that brought millions of single mothers off welfare and into the workforce.[6] It should be possible to form a national consensus to attempt something similar for our millions of idle, un-working, state-supported men of working age. Surely, the moral hazard of providing for them is no lower than providing for jobless single mothers who, unlike most un-working men, were largely busy raising children.

Then there is the task of drawing men with a criminal

record back into productive work life or introducing them to it for the first time. Sadly, we do not have a clue about how to do this. We basically have no idea what approaches to "reentry" work, or for whom. This remarkable national ignorance is due in part to a simple oversight: our statistical systems do not regularly collect social or economic information on ex-prisoners or felons in society at large (the "civilian noninstitutional population"). When that group numbered "only" a few million, as it evidently did in the early 1950s, this defect may have been understandable or excusable. But with perhaps 20 million ex-prisoners and convicted felons (the overwhelming majority of them men) now in our midst, there can be no excuse for this not-so-benign neglect. This must change, and quickly, so that we can begin to develop evidence-based approaches, public and private, to raising work rates for criminals who have paid their debts to society. A great deal of local experimentation will be in order here, and we face a steep learning curve. But the economic redemption of former prisoners and convicts is not only a pragmatic objective: it is an ennobling moral goal for a forgiving people.

While nearly all the details remain to be worked out, I can perhaps dispel one not-unreasonable worry in advance: the "menace to society" concern from bringing jobless former criminals back into the workforce. Public safety concerns are not only legitimate, but a paramount government priority. It's worth remembering, however, that the huge increase in America's ex-prisoner and at-large felon population over the past generation coincided with a dramatic drop in rates for both violent crime and property crime.[7] At the very least, this conjunction suggests that most former criminals do not pose a continuing danger to society. It should further encourage Americans to think about how we can make the most of our ex-offenders' untapped economic and social potential.

Again, these are only one person's initial thoughts and suggestions. The United States needs a broad conversation on our "men without work" problem, a conversation of many voices and differing perspectives. The urgency of the moment is to bring this invisible crisis out of the shadows and into the public spotlight. This is the indispensable first step in confronting the crisis and eventually mitigating it. As long as we allow the crisis to remain invisible, we can expect it to continue and even to worsen.

PART 2

≥≤

Dissenting Points of View

CHAPTER 11

Creating the Beginning of an End

≽≼

Henry Olsen

WINSTON CHURCHILL once told the British people that he had nothing to offer them but "blood, sweat, toil, and tears." The peril America faces from the growing epidemic of men without work pales in comparison to what the Nazi Luftwaffe posed to Britian, but I felt the same sense of dread and resolve after reading Nick Eberstadt's chapters. He painstakingly shows that there is a serious problem afoot in our land, that it is unusual to our land, and that it poses monetary and spiritual problems for our land. Yet he offers naught but the resolve that it must be fixed without giving us much of a guide as to how it might be.

To fix a problem, we must know more than what it is; we must know how it came to be, so that we may attack the problem's causes rather than its symptoms. Nick (full disclosure, a former colleague of mine at the American Enterprise Institute) does an excellent job defining what the problem is: men who can work, who choose not to work, and who spend their time doing little but entertaining themselves, usually in the purely private pursuits such as watching television. I think he falls short, however, of giving us a clear picture of how this came about. He overestimates the causative effect of government safety net programs in luring these men out of the workforce and underestimates the causative effect a changing labor market has had on the work and remuneration prospects for prime-age men, especially those without college degrees.

To see why I say this, let's start with a basic understanding of the data Nick presents. He places great stock in the labor force participation rate (LFPR) as a measure of male engagement with the workplace. That is surely the right measure to use, for if you are neither employed nor seeking work, you are by definition disengaged with the world of work. But the LFPR is calculated in a negative fashion; it is the residual from the monthly survey of the Bureau of Labor Statistics to ascertain the unemployment rate. If you tell the survey taker that you are neither employed full- or part-time and you are not currently seeking work, the Labor Department deems you outside the labor force, regardless of how you might have answered that question were it posed directly. Thus this statistic tells us that a man *is* disconnected, but it tells us nothing about the mindset of the men who *are* disconnected.

The problem of the discouraged worker gets to the heart of this. The Bureau of Labor Statistics asks workers if they are discouraged at their failure to find work and, hence, are no longer seeking it. People who say they are discouraged are counted as out of the labor force, but it is clear that these people are of a different character than those physically unable to work or those who simply choose not to work. If, for example, a man released from prison in year one cannot find a job for months after his release, he might choose to drop out of the labor force as he feels his quest is hopeless. That person can be reached in a different manner and is dropping out for a different reason than the nineteen-year-old who has been receiving Supplemental Security Insurance disability payments since he was a child and would forgo a low but steady income if he were to engage with the world of work. Failure to parse the nonworking men into these different categories means that the reader is less equipped to take up the challenge Nick poses us in chapter 9 than if that reader was in possession of such information.

The data Nick presents gives tantalizing clues that the problem of male nonwork is in fact largely a problem of repeated failure to find reasonably remunerative work, rather than a problem of the lure of ready, steady cash from Uncle Sam. To see this more clearly, we need to parse the data he presents of prime-age men who are employed, which we find in figure 2.1.

This figure presents the employment-to-population ratio for men ages twenty-five–to–fifty-four between 1948 and 2016. The employment-to-population ratio is what it seems to be: the share of the total population group sampled that is employed, full or part-time, at the time of the survey. A quick perusal of the chart shows peaks and valleys, which correspond nicely with periods of recession (valleys) and recovery. The valleys never drop below 90 percent during the twenty-seven-year period from 1948 to 1975. The 1974–75 recession, caused in part by the shock generated by the Arab oil embargo in late 1973, was particularly deep. What is telling, however, is not that the valley was deep but that the peak that followed was lower than that observed in any other recovery prior. The employment peak, observed right before the next recession of 1979, showed about 91 percent of prime-age men were employed. This was roughly 4 percent lower than the peak observed throughout the period prior to the recession of 1970 and was lower than the peak which followed that short, shallow recession.

This suggests that the twin shocks of the early 1970s coincided with a permanent 4 percent reduction in prime-age male employment. While entitlements were expanding throughout this period, there is no clear demarcation related to a particular entitlement or welfare expansion that can explain this drop. What appears to have happened is that a large percentage of prime-age males were pushed out of the workforce in recessionary periods and never came back.

This same pattern of push and dropout persists throughout the subsequent thirty-five years. Each recession following the 1979 one shows a drop in the employment-to-population ratio, which we would expect, but each one is followed by a recovery with an employment peak lower than the one immediately preceding. Even the nearly twenty-year Reagan-

Clinton expansionary period showed a peak prime-age male employment-to-population ratio of about 90 percent, or about 5 percent lower than the peak that pertained during the 1948–73 period.

This is a time of the deindustrialization of America. Manufacturing is closing down or streamlining, and the jobs that are being created are jobs for which less-well-educated, native-born males have no comparative advantage over females or, in many cases, less-well-educated immigrants. But the post-1999 period shows just how relevant these developments are.

The recession of the early 2000s was relatively mild in aggregate terms, but it was devastating to prime-age male employment. The employment-to-population ratio drops to around 87 percent but does not climb much during the mid-2000s recovery. The employment-to-population ratio peak during the Bush years is lower than *any EPR valley* in the prior fifty years, save for the depths of the 1981 recession, when unemployment rose above 10 percent. Then the 2008 crash came, and the prime-age male employment-to-population ratio plummeted more sharply than in any prior recession, even those in which national unemployment was roughly comparable to that of the 2008–10 period. Despite five years of recovery, the prime-age employment-to-population ratio is still below the lowest percentage ever recorded in any recession since 1948.

These figures are not consistent with an "entitlement pulls men out of working" hypothesis. They are consistent with an "economic changes push men out of working" hypothesis, with one small but important caveat. That caveat is that once men feel they cannot reenter the workforce, they need something to live on. Here is where entitlements play a crucial role. When jobs that pay enough to meet their skills, work history, and expectations are not present in their neighborhoods, the existence of safety-net programs provides a tempting alternative. Men on the economic margin, faced with a choice of working at an unpleasant job for a low and unsteady paycheck or not working and receiving disability for a low but steady paycheck, increasingly find the lure of the dole attractive.

A simple look at Social Security Disability Insurance (SSDI) applications and enrollments confirms this hypothesis. SSDI applications soared during the recession of the early 2000s, breaking 2 million applications per year during that period. The total number of applications never dropped appreciably even during the mid-decade recovery. Annual SSDI applications had never risen above 2 million prior to the early 2000s recession. It has never dropped below that number since.

This trend exacerbated during the Great Recession. Annual applications rose above 3 million per year immediately following the financial crash. As with last decade's recession, the total number has dropped but remains above the prior annual high. Some, but only some, of this can be explained by the aging of the workforce. The sharp rise and slow decline in applications is more consistent with the theory that men on the margin jump to whatever lifeboat they can find when the economic ship they are sailing on sinks.

This theory also explains why nonemployment is lower among immigrant prime-age males. This group includes a large number who are not here legally and for whom applying for government benefits risks discovery and deportation. Add to this their lower economic expectations, having come from nations whose standard of living is light years behind ours, and their shorter period of residency during which they have not had the time to build up the capital costs of living (house, debt payments, etc.), which increase the earnings floor one must reach to avoid going backward. They are much more free to take the jobs that are available for them because they have fewer alternatives to fall back on, and have a lower standard of living to support with the new wage.

If this is what is going on for a significant number of prime-age males, then the potential solutions to prime-age male nonwork are both much harder and more administratively complex than if the problem is simply one of lazy men of low character mooching off the rest of us. This is not to say there are not other issues to deal with. The problem of incarcerated males returning to the community presents a different and challenging issue. The problem of males who receive Supplemental Security Insurance as children and remain eligible when they turn eighteen presents another, difficult problem.

Yet another issue is presented by the post–Cold War reduction in the size of the U.S. military. The military is primarily a bastion of employment for the lower-skilled male. In the early 1960s, before the Vietnam War buildup, over 2.7 million Americans were uniformed military personnel. Today, only about 1.5 million serve in the military.[1] While many of these men are eighteen to twenty-four years of age, it's clear that the military used to take a very large share of low-skilled men out of the civilian labor force, both giving these men skills and references that could help them obtain jobs when they reentered the workforce as well as reducing competition for jobs for those men who remained civilians. The existence of the draft between 1948 and 1972 was surely an important factor in keeping "civilian" prime-age male work rates so high during that period.

If the nature of the labor market has significantly changed since the golden age of prime-age male employment, then the task of increasing male engagement with the labor force is much tougher than if we are faced with a relatively simple question of slackers gaming a too generous system. As Nick notes, the solution to this problem will require skill, dedication, and ingenuity. Those qualities are more needed if the world that society wants men to reengage with is one that doesn't really want them in the first place.

Nearly two years after the Battle of Britain began, after two years of toil and sweat had produced the British victory over Rommel's Afrika Korps at El Alamein, Churchill told the British people that they now faced not the beginning of the end, but the end of the beginning. Three more long years of blood and tears would follow before the evil that was Hitler's Germany perished in the flames of his own Gotterdammerung. Nick's work does not represent the end of the beginning of the battle against male retreat from the adult world of work, but it does represent an important step forward. Let us all dedicate ourselves to completing and extending his work so that we have a full understanding of the etiology of nonwork. This would constitute our "end of the beginning" and allow us to focus on the crucial work of creating the beginning of the end.

CHAPTER 12

A Well-Known Problem

≥≤

Jared Bernstein

NICHOLAS EBERSTADT HAS written an important analysis of a serious problem ailing the U.S. economy. The increasing share of American men disconnected from our labor force costs us economic output and lowers the household incomes of these men. It can also be psychologically damaging, given the importance that work plays in our culture and individual self-esteem.

Nick's analysis is also timely, coming as it does amid a presidential election in which an allegedly "angry working class" is rejecting establishment precepts, most notably globalization. Certainly, the lack of meaningful, gainful employment is thought to be part of this phenomenon.

MEN WITHOUT WORK IS A WELL-KNOWN PROBLEM

The problem of prime-age men without work is real, but it is not, as Nick argues, underappreciated. Labor economists have long worried about this trend, and the issue broke out of the halls of academia at least twice in the last thirty years. In the 1980s, ballooning trade deficits with lower-wage countries, the loss of U.S. manufacturing jobs, and exit of displaced American production workers from the labor force began to alarm industrial workers, their unions, and local communities. A decade ago, two *New York Times* reporters wrote on the missing-men problem.[1] It is fascinating and depressing to return to that story, since it contains most elements of Nick's analysis.

Moreover, as our current recovery has progressed and unemployment dropped, it has been widely recognized that labor force participation has significantly lagged. Economists and commentators from the CNBC crowd to the Federal Reserve have given it wide attention on the first Friday of each month ("jobs day"). As Nick himself notes, President Obama's Council of Economic Advisers (CEA) recently published a highly regarded piece on the issue.

I mention all this not to nitpick—or Nick-pick—but to make this point: To believe the men without work problem is underappreciated is to risk missing numerous important other debates that the decline of men's work has inspired— debates about automation, the role of immigration and globalization in displacing prime-age men, and the alarming trends in elevated death rates among white men with some of the same characteristics of the men not in the labor force (NILF) group.

PROBLEMS WITH THE DIAGNOSIS

Nick's evidence of the trends is largely sound and certainly exhaustive. He exploits many more datasets than is typical in this type of analysis. The longitudinal data he taps are a welcome addition to work in this area.

However, I have a fundamental disagreement with his diagnosis. Nick (and he's not alone here) insists that the declining trend in men's work is extremely linear. In fact, the trend is far more cyclical than his straight-line analysis suggests. While there's no question that trend lines through labor force participation rates (LFPRs) and especially employment rates for prime-age (25- to 54-year-old) men have a negative slope, there is critically important cyclical variation around that trend. That cyclical variation suggests the importance of demand-side explanations, and it is particularly pronounced for less-educated, prime-age men, the very group whom we worry most about in this debate.

Also, the fact that the baby boomers started aging out of the workforce in recent years has the potential to create unnecessary confusion in these data. In fact, most analyses, such as a recent influential paper by numerous Federal Reserve economists, argue that at least two-thirds of the recent decline in the LFPR is due to aging boomers retiring. The top line in Nick's figure 2.1 excludes retirees while the bottom line does not. Compare the upticks at the ends of the two series. For the twenty-plus series, which includes elderlies, the uptick is shallow. For the other line, prime-age workers, it is steeper, suggesting more of a cyclical response.

Consider, too, the recent positive trend in prime-age male employment rates: The series has regained two-thirds of its recent loss! This trend stands in stark contrast to Nick's "linear" argument. Figure 12.1 highlights a key point that is underemphasized in Nick's essay: the cyclicality of prime-age EPOPs. The evidence of strong cyclicality, especially for the least-advantaged/skilled men, suggests less their flight from work and more work's flight from them.

Acknowledging this cyclicality is important, but it doesn't undermine Nick's main point about the negative trend in men's work or the urgency of the problem. It does highlight, however, my other main disagreement with Nick's analysis: He believes that the "flight from work" is a more of a "supply-side" problem than is warranted. Though Nick agrees that weak labor demand is a causal factor, he discounts it compared to, say, the CEA's recent analysis. This leads, I believe, to a serious misdiagnosis.

Nick says virtually nothing about the loss of production worker and manufacturing jobs and the role of our persistent trade deficits in these losses. It is widely accepted that this shift has played a fundamental role in declining male work rates, but the word "manufacturing" comes up only once in Nick's analysis—in a quote from the CEA.

Rather than fleeing work, many prime-age workers, particularly the less-skilled, respond to the ebbs and flows of

FIGURE 12.1. THE PRIME-AGE EPOP FOR MEN IS NOT A STRAIGHT LINE. IT'S A RATCHET WITH STRONG CYCLICAL UPS AND DOWNS.

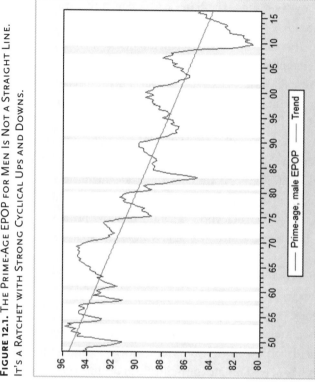

Source: Bureau of Labor Statistics and author's analysis, http://www.bls.gov.

labor demand. Nick, while recognizing demand is in the mix, downplays its importance. Part of this comes from his insufficient attention to trends in work by industry and occupation. For example, Nick argues that EPOPs for men behave differently than those for women, and he can't think of a demand-side phenomenon that would generate a difference. In fact, the shift from production work to services (think manufacturing to health care) in both the United States and other advanced economies is an excellent and well-known explanation.

Nor do I find Nick's other critiques of the demand-side explanation convincing. He argues that for those without high school degrees, immigrants have steady employment rates relative to the native born, implying that a demand-side shortfall should affect both groups. But figures from the Economic Policy Institute's *State of Working America* show that such native-born workers without a high school degree are a small and uniquely disadvantaged group. Among native-born workers, 5 percent lack a high school degree, compared to 26 percent for foreign-born workers. Nick himself underscores this point about the unique disadvantages of this small but troubled group when he points out that criminal history explains the "the remarkable gap in LFPRs between low-skilled prime-age immigrant men and low-skilled native-born men."

Also, there's an occupational story at play here, one tied, once again, to labor demand. Compared to less-educated

Hispanic immigrants, white and black high-school dropouts have not been nearly as heavily employed in construction. While the employment rates of immigrants were lifted by the sharp increase in demand for construction workers, that was less the case for black and white high school dropouts.

Finally, Nick posits that if demand-side effects were "a truly significant determinant of changes in labor force participation patterns," regional differentials would tend to diminish following such "shocks" as labor markets sought "equilibrium," and this hasn't happened. His assertion is unconvincing. Economists recognize that the nation comprises different regional labor markets that have been hit differently by trends in globalization, technology, the loss of manufacturing jobs, demography, population flows, the employment correlates of regional shocks (e.g., when the housing bubble bursts in a region with much new construction), and more. The variation Nick shows could just as easily be a function of geographical variation in labor demand as its absence.

WELFARE BENEFITS, DISABILITY, AND CRIMINAL JUSTICE

As for the causes of the American male's flight from work—an ancient left/right argument—Nick believes welfare benefits, disability, and criminal justice factors play critical roles, and gives them more weight than demand-side factors.

First, the evidence simply fails to support as strong a welfare-benefits explanation as Nick claims. It is widely agreed that our income-conditioned welfare system has become more, not less, dependent on work. The incentives increasingly go the wrong way for Nick's story. The research shows that it is almost always better to work than not to work, that marginal incentives point to the benefits of working more rather than fewer hours, and most importantly, that the safety net as a whole has little effect on the work effort of low-income workers.[2]

While Nick is on more solid ground regarding disability, both the CEA and recent work by disability expert Kathy Ruffing argue against disability insurance (DI) being a major factor in declining men's employment rates. According to the CEA, the increase in prime-age men on disability insurance is too small to explain the lion's share of the decline in work. The CEAs simulations end up assigning less than half a percentage point (out of the 7.5 points just noted) to DI, suggesting it accounts for less than 10 percent of the decline in work by these metrics.

Moreover, suppose, contrary to the CEA's findings, there were a large rise of prime-age men on disability as employment rates fall. It could easily be that jobs disappeared and these men are using disability insurance as a type of long-term unemployment insurance (a misuse, I would agree, of disability insurance). Weak labor demand could be a reason for higher disability insurance rolls rather than the disability insurance rolls being an explanation for weak labor supply.

Though Ruffing does not look exclusively at prime-age workers, she shows that population growth, aging, *and* the increase in women eligible for Social Security Disability Insurance explain much of the increase in the disability rolls. She also makes an interesting demand-side observation: while disability insurance applications spiked in the Great Recession, awards did not. This suggests that higher disability insurance rolls (applications) may be a function of weak demand for prime-age men.

What about Nick's evidence in table 8.1? Here again, there's a disconnect between his evidence and conclusion. As I read the table, it shows that prime-age men not in the labor force were more likely to receive disability and Medicaid benefits in 2013 than in 1985. But nothing in Nick's argument shows this results from prime-age men rejecting available employment and taking benefits instead. Absent that, this becomes an argument as to whether NILF men are getting too much in the way of benefits (or the wrong type of benefits).

I do agree with Nick that the large number of prime-age (and younger) men in the criminal justice system is a serious factor in the "men without work" phenomenon, especially among minority men. Incarceration rates have risen partly as a function of lengthy sentences for nonviolent crimes, nudged along with a strong dose of discrimination against nonwhites.

Even in periods of strong labor demand, these men would (and do) face high labor market barriers.

WHAT'S TO BE DONE?

Nick's analysis of the problem is one of the most exhaustive I have seen. His solutions, however, fall short. After several pages of diagnosis, we get minimal prescription. That's unfortunate, given the welcome urgency Nick brings to the subject.

Nick's first solution is more entrepreneurialism, though he does not suggest how to achieve this. More business creation would surely help job creation. But economists have few explanations as to why business startup rates are low.

I clearly disagree with Nick's "work first" ideas. I see no good coming from making these programs less generous or further conditioning them on work. Essentially, I think Nick makes the same mistake that other conservatives make in assuming that, if poor people wanted a job, they could get one. Not every prime-age, nonworking male is poor, of course, but they are disproportionately low-income and less educated, and often face steep barriers to labor market entry, including criminal records and racial discrimination. Researchers at the Georgetown Center on Poverty and Inequality recently published a comprehensive examination of subsidized employment programs that have consistently seen high rates of voluntary participation over the past forty years. They report that the "number of disadvantaged people willing to work consistently exceeds the number in competitive employment."

Policy can achieve stronger labor demand conditions. The CEA offers several recommendations (expanding the Earned Income Tax Credit for childless workers, higher minimum wages, paid leave, and child care assistance). The agenda I lay out in my recent book, *The Reconnection Agenda*, emphasizes pro-work/full employment fiscal and monetary policies, lowering the trade deficit and, perhaps most important here, direct job creation. As long as there is a surfeit of takers for such programs and they have a good track record, I see no downside at all to significantly expanding their footprint with resource streams. Perhaps all of us who are concerned about men without work can agree that this is a useful way forward, even as we debate the relative roles of supply-side and demand-side factors.

Finally, those on all sides of the political aisle agree that criminal justice reform is integral to solving the men without work problem. Such reforms must focus both on reducing individuals' exposure to the criminal justice system and mitigating the effects of that exposure, through policing and sentencing reforms, expanding alternatives to incarceration, and "fair chance" hiring policies that protect these men from labor market discrimination.

CHAPTER 13

A Response to Olsen and Bernstein

≽≼

Nicholas Eberstadt

MY THANKS to Jared and Henry for kicking off this discussion, and debate with such thoughtful observations and criticisms. I very much appreciate the kind words they offer for some of this research.

We three seem to be largely in agreement about the dimensions and contours of the "men without work" problem but disagree (at times acutely) about diagnoses of the problem and prescriptions for remedying it. So let's focus on some of these contested areas.

Jared suggests the men-without-work problem is already well known. Maybe to a couple of dozen labor economists at think tanks and universities and to a similar number of business reporters and economics bloggers. Yet to more or less everyone else in the country, this is indeed, as I asserted in my subtitle, a largely "invisible" crisis—and "everyone else" includes most policymakers in Washington. If well-informed people really understood the magnitude of the male "flight from work" phenomenon, why would the "unemployment rate" still be the banner headline for virtually every story on each new monthly employment report? As I show in chapter 3, for every prime-age man who is out of a job and looking for one there are three others who are neither working nor looking for work.

Jared (and also Henry) strenuously object that my account places far too little weight on the role of "demand-side" factors (not least among these, the dramatic postwar decline in U.S. manufacturing jobs, partly or largely as a consequence of foreign trade competition) in creating America's men-without-work problem. Please note, I do not contest at all the proposition that a lack of demand for male labor, and especially less-skilled male labor, is one of the factors responsible for today's dire situation. I expressly agree with that proposition, and repeatedly, in chapter 7. My point rather is that demand factors are only one part of the dynamic: "supply" and "institutional" factors are the others. The real question here, then, is the relative importance of these respective factors.

I argue that institutional factors (i.e., the detachment from the labor force of many in America's huge new army of male ex-prisoners and felons) is a significant and generally underappreciated component of today's men-without-work problem (chapter 9), and I do not read Jared or Henry as contesting this. So the residual dispute must turn on the weight, within the overall postwar collapse of male work, of (1) a lack of jobs per se on the one hand and (2) a lack of motivation to engage in the competition for jobs on the other.

Men Without Work outlines five reasons that demand factors could well be less powerful in explaining the collapse of male work in modern America than many labor economists today assume (see chapter 7). Since I do not explicitly deal with the issue of manufacturing job decline—as Jared and Henry both fault me for and in retrospect I'd say quite correctly—let me add a sixth here: namely, there is some evidence of a relatively weak relationship between the decline in manufacturing jobs and the prime-age male flight from work for advanced Western countries as a whole over the postwar era.

Figure 13.1 makes the case. Between 1970 and 2012, manufacturing jobs as a share of total employment in the United States dropped by about sixteen percentage points, to just over 10 percent. But that outcome was hardly unique: in France, for example, the drop was over fifteen points; in Sweden, sixteen points; in Australia sixteen points. France and Sweden follow closely the United States' "de-industrial" trend line, and Australia now has a markedly lower share of employment in manufacturing than America—yet trends in labor force participation for prime-age men in the United States were uniquely disappointing when compared to other rich Western societies. Why this unwelcome "American exceptionalism"? Whatever the reason, it's not because

FIGURE 13.1 PERCENTAGE OF TOTAL EMPLOYMENT IN MANUFACTURING, 1970–2012: UNITED STATES AND SELECTED OTHER COUNTRIES

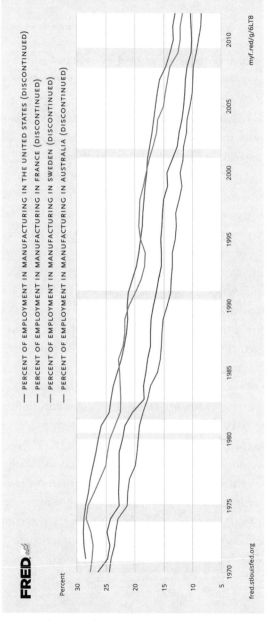

— PERCENT OF EMPLOYMENT IN MANUFACTURING IN THE UNITED STATES (DISCONTINUED)
— PERCENT OF EMPLOYMENT IN MANUFACTURING IN FRANCE (DISCONTINUED)
— PERCENT OF EMPLOYMENT IN MANUFACTURING IN SWEDEN (DISCONTINUED)
— PERCENT OF EMPLOYMENT IN MANUFACTURING IN AUSTRALIA (DISCONTINUED)

myf.red/g/6LT8

fred.stlouisfed.org

Source: Federal Reserve Economic Data, Federal Reserve Bank of St. Louis, https://fred.stlouisfed.org, Accessed August 24, 2016.

other advanced economies weren't undergoing big structural transformations, too.

To highlight some disagreements over the role of welfare and disability programs: nowhere do I claim these *caused* the male flight from work. My argument instead is that they *financed* it—and in much larger measure than many researchers seem to appreciate. As I show in chapter 8, over half of prime-age men not in the labor force are themselves getting money from at least one government disability program nowadays, as are two-thirds of prime-age males not in the labor force (NILF) households. Making the case that most of the growth in Social Security Disability Insurance (SSDI) enrollment is explained by other demographic variables does not vitiate that finding—much less the fact that the share of prime-age men on SSDI has more than tripled over the past half century. Note incidentally that geographic mobility in America has fallen sharply over that same period, meaning, inter alia, that dependent men without work are less likely to move to higher-work states. Any dots to connect here?

As to policy recommendations: I was deliberately sparing of these for a number of reasons, not least because I did not want to propose an agenda I would have favored in advance, and for other reasons, under the guise of addressing the troubles identified in this study.

For job generation, my preferences favor revitalization of small business, while Jared's may be for a public hand: I will grant him that his is the easier to effect by governmental decree. In regard to my call for disability reform: Is there really anyone left in Washington who doesn't know the U.S. disability system is badly broken? My proposed "work first" principle for public aid for working-age men is channeling not Charles Dickens but rather contemporary Sweden, with its highly effective social policy changes over the past generation. I should have thought Jared would be sympathetic to those.

If we could succeed in reforming welfare for un-working single mothers twenty years ago, why not for un-working men today? Perhaps because the U.S. economy is weaker? A reasonable objection. But a key study on that earlier success concluded that macroeconomic conditions played only a relatively small role in getting women back in the labor force, with changes in incentives accomplishing most of that feat instead.[1]

Two Final Comments in Response to Henry

First, his observation about the role of the draft in augmenting skills and training for young men in the early postwar era, while politically incorrect, may be very much on target. Remember, though, that the "selective service" was indeed selective—and as late as the Kennedy administration, one-third of the young men tested failed either physical or cognitive requirements for service. (That finding was ammunition, so to speak, for the Johnson administration's "war on poverty.") Thus, the most disadvantaged were also the least likely to avail themselves of such employment-enhancing experience as military conscription could provide.

And I am in violent agreement with Henry's lament that available data can "tell us that a man *is* disconnected" from the labor force, but "tells us nothing about the mindset of the men who *are* disconnected." Henry puts his finger on not only a failure of government information systems but a failure of empathy and understanding in our nation—perhaps a failure of mobility and solidarity as well. Would intellectuals and decision-makers in the early postwar era have been so obviously out of touch with "how the other half lives" as they are today? I have my doubts. Illuminating this human dimension of "America's invisible crisis" should be imperative—not only for the instrumental reason of addressing a social ill, but for the moral one: we are a humane society, and this is exactly the sort of thing a humane society should want to know.

Notes

≳≲

CHAPTER 1

1. Also, please note that wealth hit a new record in June 2016, according to a Federal Reserve report: Josh Zumbrun, "According to Federal Reserve Report," *Wall Street Journal*, June 9, 2016, http://www.wsj.com/articles/americans-total-wealth-hits-record-according-to-federal-reserve-report-1465488231.

2. "Global Wealth Databook 2015," table 6.1, Credit Suisse, last modified October 2015, http://publications.credit-suisse.com/tasks/render/file/index.cfm?fileid=C26E3824-E868-56E0-CCA04D4BB9B9ADD5.

3. August 2016 projections for 2016–2026 by Congressional Budget Office anticipates full potential growth for U.S. GDP. See Congressional Budget Office, "Budget and Economic Data: Potential GDP and Underlying Inputs," https://www/cbo.gov/about/products/budget_economic_data#6. It is possible that the anemic state of the U.S. macroeconomy is being exaggerated by measurement issues—productivity improvements from information technology, for example, have been oddly elusive in our officially reported national output—but few today imagine that such concealed gains would totally transform our view of the real economy's true performance.

4. Carmen M. Reinhart and Kenneth S. Rogoff, "Recovery from Financial Crises: Evidence from 100 Episodes," *American Economic Review: Papers and Proceedings* 104, no. 5: 50–55. http://scholar.harvard.edu/files/rogoff/files/aer_104-5_50-55.pdf.

5. Cf. Robert J. Gordon, *The Rise and Fall of American Growth: The U.S. Standard of Living since the Civil War* (Princeton, NJ: Princeton University Press, 2016); see for example, Lawrence H. Summers, "U.S.

Economic Prospects: Secular Stagnation, Hysteresis, and the Zero Lower Bound," *Business Economics* 49, no. 2: 65–73.

6. August 2016 projections for 2016–2026 by Congressional Budget Office anticipates full potential growth for U.S. GDP. See Congressional Budget Office, "Budget And Economic Data: Potential GDP and Underlying Inputs," https://www.cbo.gov/about/products/budget_economic_data#6.

7. Simple calculations based on Bureau of Labor Statistics numbers make the point. If the employment to population ratio for those twenty and older were as high in early 2016 as it had been in the year 2000, an additional 9.7 million Americans would be at work today. And this is a net estimate that takes into account the fact that work rates have been going up for our rapidly growing population of senior citizens. For adults between the ages of twenty and sixty-five, the number of people engaged in paid labor in early 2016 was roughly 12.5 million people fewer than would have been the case if work rates from 2000 still prevailed. Estimates derived from BLS, "Labor Force Statistics from the Current Population Survey," http://data.bls.gov/pdq/query tool.jsp?survey=ln.

8. The sharp decline in work by and for Americans in the early twenty-first century is also underscored by estimates of the sheer volume of work done. According to the Bureau of Economic Analysis (BEA), total hours worked by full- and part-time American employees rose by less than 4 percent between 2000 and 2014 (the latest year available; see "NIPA Tables," table 6.9D, Bureau of Economic Analysis, http://www.bea.gov/iTable/iTable.cfm?ReqID=9#reqid=9&step=1&isuri=1). Over those same years, the civilian noninstitutional adult population twenty-plus years of age grew by almost 18 percent, and the twenty-plus labor force grew by nearly 12 percent (see Labor Force Statistics from the Current Population Survey, Series LNU00000024 and LNU01000024, http://data.bls.gov/pdq/querytool.jsp?survey=ln).

9. This number plunged from 70 percent in early 2000 to 23 percent in 2014, according to one major public opinion survey. Cf. http://www.gallup.com/poll/175793/no-change-mood-satisfied-not.aspx. On the large majorities of Americans who still regard America as being stuck in recession; see, for instance, Elizabeth Thom, "New Survey Reveals

an Anxious and Nostalgic America Going into the 2016 Election,"
Brookings Institution, last modified November 18, 2015, https://
www.brookings.edu/2015/11/18/new-survey-reveals-an-anxious-and-
nostalgic-america-going-into-the-2016-election/.

Chapter 2

1. Joe Weisenthal, "The Jobless Numbers Aren't Just Good, They're Great,"
Bloomberg video, 1:21, August 6, 2015, http://www.bloomberg.com
/news/videos/2015-08-06/the-jobless-numbers-aren-t-just-good-they
-re-great.
2. Ben Casselman, "The Jobs Report Is Even Better Than It Looks," Five
ThirtyEight, November 6, 2015, http://fivethirtyeight.com/features/
the-jobs-report-is-even-better-than-it-looks/.
3. Greg Ip, "Healthy Job Market at Odds with Global Gloom," *Wall
Street Journal*, March 30, 2016, http://www.wsj.com/articles/
healthy-job-market-at-odds-with-global-gloom-1459357330
4. Nelson D. Schwartz, "The Recovery's Two Sides," *New York Times*,
April 28, 2016, http://www.nytimes.com/2016/04/29/business/econ-
omy/us-economy-gdp-q1-growth.html?_r=0.
5. Bourree Lam, "June's Super Jobs Report", *Atlantic Monthly*, July 8
2016, http://www.theatlantic.com/business/archive/2016/07/june-jobs
-report/490466/.
6. Ben Bernanke, "How the Fed Saved the Economy," Brookings, October 4, 2015, https://www.brookings.edu/opinions/how-the-fed-saved
-the-economy/.
7. Martin Feldstein, "The U.S. Economy Is in Good Shape," *Wall
Street Journal*, February 21, 2016, http://www.wsj.com/articles/
the-u-s-economy-is-in-good-shape-1456097121.
8. Jana Raindow, Christopher Condon, and Matthew Boesler, "Yellen
Says U.S. Near Full Employment, Some Slack Remains," Bloomberg,
April 7, 2016, http://www.bloomberg.com/news/articles/2016-04-07/
yellen-says-u-s-close-to-full-employment-some-slack-remains.
9. Note that the workforce is officially defined as the sixteen-plus population (more or less is the age you legally can get out of school); historically it was the fourteen-plus population. In this study, I use three

measures working age population: twenty-plus, twenty–to–sixty-four, and the "prime working" ages of twenty-five–to– fifty-four.

10. While the U.S. Great Depression is conventionally dated as lasting from 1929 to 1939, in part to concord with the eruption of World War II that ended any peacetime economic slumps besetting European powers, unemployment data suggest that the effects of the Depression continued on into 1940 and 1941—indeed almost to our entry into that same conflict. According to the nascent test run of the present CPS, which began producing its first estimates of the U.S. employment situation in March 1940, the U.S. unemployment rate averaged nearly 11.5 percent of the civilian labor force for the first half of 1941—a higher level than ever recorded for any single month in postwar American history. As of April 12, 1941, according to these figures, the civilian unemployment rate was over 12 percent. See "Unemployment Rate for United States," FRED Economic Data, last modified August 17, 2012, https://research.stlouisfed.org/fred2/series/M0892BUSM156SNBR, and "Civilian Unemployment Rate," FRED Economic Data, last modified August 5, 2016, https://research.stlouisfed.org/fred2/series/UNRATENSA.

11. Initial CPS estimates for 1940 placed the civilian unemployment rate at an average of 14.6 percent for the months it covered. The 1940 population census put the civilian unemployment rate at 15.2 percent (see "Unemployment Rate for United States," FRED Economic Data, last modified August 17, 2012, https://research.stlouisfed.org/fred2/series/M0892BUSM156SNBR; "Census of Population and Housing," vol. 3, part 1, chapter 1, table 2, U.S. Census Bureau, http://www.census.gov/prod/www/decennial.html#y1940popv3.

12. Linda Levine, "The Labor Market during the Great Depression and the Current Recession," Congressional Research Service, last modified June 19, 2009, http://digital.library.unt.edu/ark:/67531/metadc26169/m1/1/high_res_d/R40655_2009Jun19.pdf.

13. John E. Bregger, "The Current Population Survey: A Historical Perspective and BLS' Role," *Monthly Labor Review* (June 1984): 8–14. http://www.bls.gov/opub/mlr/1984/06/art2full.pdf.

14. Note, incidentally, that our current decade's level is four percentage points higher than the corresponding estimate for prime-age men from

the 1940 census—and the current decade's work rate for men twenty–to–sixty-four is over two points lower than for their counterparts back in 1940. Our current decade's work rates would look even worse if we compared them instead to the levels reported in the 1930 census.

15. This is calculated on the ten-year cohort of twenty-five–to–sixty-four and the five-year cohort of twenty to twenty-four.

16. Robert Zemsky and Daniel Shapiro, "On Measuring a Mirage: Why U.S. Training Numbers Don't Add Up" (working paper, National Center on the Educational Quality of the Workforce, Washington, DC), http://files.eric.ed.gov/fulltext/ED372191.pdf.

17. Derived from "CPS Historical Time Series Tables on School Enrollment," U.S. Census Bureau, http://www.census.gov/hhes/school/data/cps/historical/.

18. According to the Census Bureau CPS data, the matrix of school enrollment and employment for men twenty and older in the United States in 2014 looked like this:

Age	Total	Employed	Unemployed	Discouraged— Not in Labor Force (NILF)	Other— Not in Labor Force (NILF)
20+	7,028,145	3,884,208	257,545	39,641	2,846,751
20–24	4,045,022	1,841,584	126,263	27,258	2,049,918
25–54	2,847,750	1,970,127	129,208	12,383	736,032
55–64	103,634	57,518	2,074	0	44,042
65+	31,739	14,979	0	0	16,760

Derived by Alex Coblin of the American Enterprise Institute from the October 2014 CPS microdata especially for this study.

19. And not all of this schooling is directly or even indirectly employment related.

CHAPTER 3

1. On this great transformation, see, among many others, Claudia Gol-
din, "The Quiet Revolution That Transformed Women's Employment,
Education, and Family," *APA Papers and Proceedings* (May 2006):
1–21. http://scholar.harvard.edu/files/goldin/files/the_quiet_revolu
tion_that_transformed_womens_employment_education_and_family.
pdf?m=1360041519.

2. In 2015 the Census Bureau's ASEC survey from the CPS reported that
just 15 percent of prime-age men who were out of the labor force for
the whole previous year gave "could not find work" as the reason. See
"POV-24. Reason for Not Working or Reason for Spending Time Out
of the Labor Force—Poverty Status of People Who Did Not Work or
Who Spent Time Out of the Labor Force," U.S. Census Bureau, last
modified May 5, 2016, http://www.census.gov/data/tables/time-series/
demo/income-poverty/cps-pov/pov-24.2014.html#.html

3. Note these are annual averages for monthly figures—point in time
estimates, rather than estimates for the numbers of men completely
out of the workforce for the totality of the calendar year.

4. For the broader twenty–to–sixty-four years of age, there were already
well over twice as many un-working as unemployed men in 1965, and
by 2015, there were well over four times as many. Even in the worst
of the Great Recession, out-of-work men in the twenty–to–sixty-four
bracket were far outnumbered by un-working men (roughly 9 million
vs. roughly 15 million in early 2010).

5. This data seems to have been purged from the Census Bureau, the
National Bureau of Economic Research, Integrated Public Use Microdata Sets, and the Library of Congress. It's a cautionary tale for our
data-rich era!

6. We cannot readily calculate the corresponding proportion in 1948
because the Census Bureau online historical data series for annual CPS-
based estimates of age- and sex-specific enrollments only extend back
to 1961. See "School Enrollment Reports and Tables from Previous
Years," U.S. Census Bureau, http://www.census.gov/hhes/school/data/
cps/previous/index.html.

CHAPTER 4

1. Robert William Fogel et al., *Political Arithmetic: Simon Kuznets and the Empirical Tradition in Economics* (Chicago: University of Chicago Press, 2013), introduction, http://www.nber.org/chapters/c12912.pdf.

2. Dora L. Costa, "The Wage and the Length of the Work Day: From the 1890s to 1991" (working paper, National Bureau of Economic Research, Cambridge, MA, April 1998), http://www.nber.org/papers/w6504.

3. Dora L. Costa, *The Evolution of Retirement: An American Economic History, 1880-1990*, (Chicago: University of Chicago Press, 1998), chapter 2.

4. This upsurge also coincided with a marriage boom and a baby boom—meaning that men may not only have been more capable of entering the labor market, but more motivated to do so as well.

5. Derived from the Human Mortality Database: http:www.mortality.org.

6. "Percent of People 25 Years and Over Who Have Completed High School or College," by Race, Hispanic Origin, and Sex: Selected Years 1940 to 2015, U.S. Census Bureau, https://www.census.gov/hhes/socdemo/education/data/cps/historical/tabA-2.xlsx.

7. Roughly similar rankings within this same grouping of countries prevailed among U.S. women with respect to LFPRs. In 2014, U.S. females ranked, out of twenty-three countries, twenty-first for those ages twenty-five-to–fifty-four, seventeenth for those ages fifteen–to–sixty-four, tenth for those ages fifty-five–to–sixty-four, and third for those ages sixty-five and older.

8. "OECD Economic Policy Reforms: Going for Growth 2016," OECD, http://www.oecd.org/eco/goingforgrowth.htm and also "Social Expenditure Database," OECD, http://www.oecd.org/social/expenditure.htm.

9. "GDP Per Capita, PPP (Constant 2011 International $)," World Bank, http://data.worldbank.org/indicator/NY.GDP.PCAP.PP.KD.

10. There is research suggesting that OECD figures may understate the U.S. and Europe divergence: See Alexander Bick, Bettina Brüggemann, and Nicola Fuchs-Schündeln, "Hours Worked in Europe and the US: New

Data, New Answers," (unpublished manuscript, July 5, 2016), http://www.wiwi.uni-frankfurt.de/profs/fuchs/staff/fuchs/paper/bbf_hours.pdf.

11. Juliet Schor, *The Overworked American: The Unexpected Decline of Leisure* (New York: Basic Books, 1992).

12. http://gutenberg.ca/ebooks/keynes-essaysinpersuasion/keynes-essaysinpersuasion-00-h.html.

CHAPTER 5

1. Trends were even worse for the widowed prime-age men—but this was and still is a tiny group, comprising less than 1 percent of the total civilian noninstitutional population.

2. So great are these gaps in LFPRs between less-educated native-born and foreign-born men, and so steep have been the declines in workforce participation for less-educated American men over the past two generations, that one is almost tempted to wonder if some systematic failure of public kindergarten-through-twelfth-grade education accounts for these extraordinary results. We will identify other factors besides—or perhaps we should say, in addition to—any mounting problems the U.S. primary and secondary school systems may have experienced that could help to explain the collapse of work among less-educated American men in recent times.

CHAPTER 6

1. Josef Pieper, *Leisure: The Basis of Culture* (San Francisco: Ignatius Press, 2009).

2. Max Weber, *The Protestant Ethic and the Spirit of Capitalism*, trans. (Mineola, NY: Dover, 2003), p. 157.

3. William H. Beveridge, *Full Employment in a Free Society: A Report* (Abingdon, England: Routledge, 2015), 18, 19.

4. Mai Weismantle, "Reasons People Do Not Work: 1996: Household Economic Studies," *Current Population Reports* (2001), table 3, http://www.census.gov/prod/2001pubs/p70-76.pdf.

5. Nasrin Dalirazar, "Reasons People Do Not Work: 2004: Household

Economic Studies," *Current Population Reports* (2007), table 3, https://www.census.gov/prod/2007pubs/p70-111.pdf.

6. The current annual ATUS draws its respondents out of the CPS interview pool as they complete their rotation there. Since 2003, the survey has been conducted annually, and in recent years its sample size has averaged about 26,000 persons ages fifteen or older. The ATUS was also conducted two earlier times—in 1965–66 and in 1985—by the Survey Research Center at the University of Michigan. These had much smaller sample sizes, but in the case of the 1965–66 survey much higher response rates. The current ATUS has had annual response rates within its sample in the 50 to 60 percent range, as against a response rate of more than 80 percent for the 1965–66 survey. For more information, see "Original Data Included," Centre for Time Use Research, http://www.timeuse.org/sites/ctur/files/819/ahtus-original-data-19-july-2013.pdf; *American Time Use Survey User's Guide: Understanding ATUS 2003 to 2015* (Washington, DC: Bureau of Labor Statistics, 2016), http://www.bls.gov/tus/atususersguide.pdf; and Mark Aguiar and Erik Hurst, *The Increase in Leisure Inequality: 1965–2005* (Washington, DC: AEI Press, 2009), appendix, http://www.aei.org/wp-content/uploads/2014/03/-increase-in-leisure-inequality_095714451042.pdf.

7. Aguiar and Hurst, *Increase in Leisure Inequality*.

8. Which they refer to as "leisure"—but we do not in this study, insofar as we argue that the label prejudges the actual outcome of the nonwork under consideration.

9. Aguiar and Hurst, *Increase in Leisure Inequality*, 59–60.

10. Cf. Lisa K. Schwartz, "The American Time Use Survey: Cognitive Pretesting," *Monthly Labor Review* (February 2002): 34–44. http://www.bls.gov/opub/mlr/2002/02/art2full.pdf.

11. An early exposition of the concept of "time poverty" may be found in Clair Vickery, "The Time Poor: A New Look at Poverty," *Journal of Human Resources* 12, no. 1 (Winter 1977): 27–48, http://www.jstor.org/stable/145597.

12. This does not necessarily mean that prime-age NILF women are not devoting much of their time to caring for others. As we already saw from SIPP figures, in both 1996 and 2004 nearly 40 percent of women between the ages of twenty–and–sixty-four who were not working for

four consecutive months stated that the main reason they were not at work was caregiving.

13. At this point we must mention the disability problem. Some considerable fraction of the prime-age men who neither work nor seek work happen to suffer from disabilities. There are many different survey-based estimates of the scope and severity of physical and mental limitations on the part of working-age men and women in modern America—not all of them consistent with one another. All of these surveys indicate that un-working prime-age men report higher levels of disability than working men or women—and generally speaking, higher rates of disability than unemployed men as well. The ASEC 2015, for example, reports that 47 percent of the prime-age men who did not work at all in 2014 said this was because they were ill or disabled, "Reason for Not Working or Reason for Spending Time out of the Labor Force— Poverty Status of People Who Did Not Work or Who Spent Time out of the Labor Force," U.S. Census Bureau, http://www.census.gov/data/ tables/2015/demo/cps/pov-24.html#par_textimage_10

We will deal with the disability question in more detail later in this book. It is surely the case that differential burdens of disability have some impact on differences in time use for the four groups in table 6.1. That said, it is also apparent that differential rates of disability cannot account for most or even much of the discrepancies between NILF men and all the others with respect to helping at home or in the community.

Consider the following thought experiment. Assume that one-quarter of NILF men suffered such serious limitations as to restrict their capability to perform any care for others, engage in religious activity, or volunteer out of the home but that the others were as functional as working men and women their same ages. Assume further that those three-fourths of prime-age NILF men spent the same amount of time in personal care, eating/drinking, and on "socializing, relaxing, and leisure" as working men and women. And assume that the nondisabled NILF men expended the same fraction of their remaining postwork time at these "helping" activities as do working men and women. What would this mean for their time budgets and for the availability of time to help others for the NILF group as a whole?

The assumption that one-quarter of the NILF group is completely incapable of home care, care for others, volunteering, etc., is, we should note, an extremely strong one. (We should further bear in mind that prime-age working men and women also can and do live with disabilities—and those disability burdens are already reflected in the time survey in table 6.1.) That said, by these assumptions, expected overall NILF time expenditure levels for home care and community activities would be more than 75 percent higher than the level for employed men. For employed women, the corresponding differential would be 45 percent. As we have already seen, actual overall daily time expenditures by NILF men were far below these notional contra-factual levels.

14. As the Bureau of Labor Statistics webpage on frequently asked questions about the ATUS explains: "The American Time Use Survey (ATUS) is not a good source of information about how people use the Internet. Activities are coded based on how survey respondents were using the Internet, not whether they were using this tool. For example, if a respondent reports 'ordering groceries online,' this activity would be assigned the activity code for 'grocery shopping.' If a respondent reports 'updating my blog,' the activity would be coded as 'writing for personal interest.' The category 'computer use for leisure (excluding games)' includes some Internet use, but it is not comprehensive and it also includes non-Internet-based activities."

See "Frequently Asked Questions," Bureau of Labor Statistics, last modified August 3, 2016, http://www.bls.gov/tus/atusfaqs.htm#24.

15. Since 1972, the GSS has been collecting a wide array of attitudinal and behavioral data through personal interviews with respondents. Since 1994, these interviews have been conducted biennially, and while each wave asks hundreds of the same standard questions, new batteries of questions on particular topics are added in particular years. For more information, see "General Social Survey," NORC, http://www.norc.org/Research/Projects/Pages/general-social-survey.aspx.

16. Cf. Kory Kroft et al., "Long-Term Unemployment and the Great Recession: The Role of Composition, Duration Dependence, and Non-Participation" (working paper, National Bureau of Economc Research, Washington, DC). http://www.nber.org/papers/w20273.

17. Rand Ghayad, "The Jobless Trap," http://citeseerx.ist.psu.edu/viewdoc/download?doi=10.1.1.692.6736&rep=rep1&type=pdf.

CHAPTER 7

1. "The Long-Term Decline in Prime-Age Male Labor Force Participation," whitehouse.gov, last modified June 2016, https://www.
   whitehouse.gov/sites/default/files/page/files/20160620_cea_primeage
   _male_lfp.pdf.

2. Ibid., 26–27.

3. Donald O. Parsons, "The Decline in Male Labor Force Participation,"
   The Journal of Political Economy, Vol. 88, No. 1. (February 1980),
   pp. 117—34; Chinhui Juhn "Decline of Male Labor Market Participation: The Role of Declining Market Opportunities," The Quarterly
   Journal of Economics, Vol. 107, No. 1 (Feb., 1992), pp. 79–121, Published by Oxford University Press, Stable URL: http://www.jstor.org
   /stable/211832.

4. Ravi Balakrishnan et al., "Recent U.S. Labor Force Dynamics," (working paper, International Monetary Fund, Washington, DC). https://
   www.imf.org/external/pubs/ft/wp/2015/wp1576.pdf.

5. See http://data.bls.gov/pdq/querytool.jsp?survey=ln.

CHAPTER 8

1. Bruce Meyer and Nikolas Mittag, "Using Linked Survey and Administrative Data to Better Measure Income: Implications for Poverty,
   Program Effectiveness, and Holes in the Safety Net," EconPapers, last
   modified August 7, 2016, http://econpapers.repec.org/paper/aeirpa-
   per/862403.htm.

2. See for example, Laura Wheaton, "Underreporting of Means-Tested
   Transfer Programs in the CPS and SIPP," Urban Institute, last modified February 6, 2008, http://www.urban.org/research/publication/
   underreporting-means-tested-transfer-programs-cps-and-sipp.

3. Derived from "Annual Statistical Report on the Social Security Disability Insurance Program, 2014," tables 4 and 6, Social Security Administration, last modified November 2015, https://www.ssa.gov/policy
   /docs/statcomps/di_asr/.

4. Derived from "SSI Annual Statistical Report, 2014," Social Security, last
   modified October 2015, https://www.ssa.gov/policy/docs/statcomps
   /ssi_asr/.

5. "Veterans' Disability Compensation: Trends and Policy Options," Congressional Budget Office, August 7, 2014, https://www.cbo.gov/publication/45615.

6. Cf. David H. Autor and Mark Duggan, "Supporting Work: A Proposal for Modernizing the U.S. Disability Insurance System," Center for American Progress and the Hamilton Project, last modified December 2010, http://economics.mit.edu/files/6281.

7. "The Long-Term Decline in Prime-Age Male Labor Force Participation," 20–21, whitehouse.gov, last modified June 2016, https://www.whitehouse.gov/sites/default/files/page/files/20160620_cea_primeage_male_lfp.pdf.

8. Henry Olsen, "A New Homestead Act—To Jump Start the U.S. Economy," The National Interest, last modified December 15, 2015, http://nationalinterest.org/feature/new-homestead-act%E2%80%94-jumpstart-the-us-economy-14618.

9. Michael Tanner and Charles Hughes, "The Work Versus Welfare Trade-Off: 2013 An Analysis of The Total Level of Welfare Benefits by State," (Washington DC: Cato Institute, 2013) http://object.cato.org/sites/cato.org/files/pubs/pdf/the_work_versus_welfare_trade-off_2013_wp.pdf, accessed August 1st, 2016.

10. Cf. Nicholas Eberstadt, The Poverty of "the Poverty Rate" (Washington, DC: AEI Press, 2008). https://www.aei.org/wp-content/uploads/2014/03/-the-poverty-of-the-poverty-rate_102237565852.pdf.

11. "Deciles of Income Before Taxes: Annual Expenditure Means, Shares, Standard Errors, and Coefficients of Variation, Consumer Expenditure Study," Bureau of Labor Statistics, http://www.bls.gov/cex/2014/combined/decile.pdf.

12. Derived from "Computations for the 2014 Annual Update of the HHS Poverty Guidelines for the 48 Contiguous States and the District of Columbia," Office of the Assistant Secretary for Planning and Evaluation, last modified December 1, 2014, https://aspe.hhs.gov/computations-2014-annual-update-hhs-poverty-guidelines-48-contiguous-states-and-district-columbia.

13. If noncash government benefits to these homes were taken into account for a more comprehensive measure of household consumption here, the rise in living standards for nonworkers might have been closer to

that of workers (or might actually have exceeded the rise for workers) whose real per capita level rose by 19 percent over those same years. Those calculations, however, are beyond the scope of this study.

14. "Quintiles of Income Before Taxes: Annual Expenditure Means, Shares, Standard Errors, and Coefficients of Variation, Consumer Expenditure Survey, 2014," Bureau of Labor Statistics, http://www .bls.gov/cex/2014/combined/quintile.pdf.

CHAPTER 9

1. Thomas P. Bonczar, et. al., "National Corrections Reporting Program: Time served in state prison, by offense, release type, sex, and race" 2009 edition, www.bjs.gov/data/content/ncrpto9.zip, Table 11.

2. E. Ann Carson and Daniela Golinelli, "Prisoners in 2012: Trends in Admissions and Releases, 1991–2012," table 2, Bureau of Justice Statistics, last modified September 2, 2014, http://www.bjs.gov/content/ pub/pdf/p12tar9112.pdf; E. Ann Carson, "Prisoners in 2014," table 7, Bureau of Justice Statistics, last modified September 2015, http:// www.bjs.gov/content/pub/pdf/p14.pdf.

3. Sean Rosenmerkel, Matthew Durose, and Donald Farole Jr., "Felony Sentences in State Courts, 2006—Statistical Tables," tables 1.1 and 1.2, Bureau of Justice Statistics, last modified November 22, 2010, http://www.bjs.gov/content/pub/pdf/fssco6st.pdf.

4. Christopher Uggen, Jeff Manza, and Melissa Thompson, "Citizenship, Democracy, and the Civic Reintegration of Criminal Offenders," Annals of the American Academy of Political and Social Science 605 (May 2006): 281–310, http://sociology.fas.nyu.edu/docs/IO/3858/ Citizenship,_Democracy,_and_the_Civic_Reintegration_of_Criminal_Offenders.pdf; see also Sarah K.S. Shannon, et. al., "The Growth, Scope and Spatial Distribution of America's Criminal Class, 1948–2010," unpublished paper, January 2015.

5. I cited Henry Olsen earlier in this study to the effect that welfare and social disability programs may be contributing to the increasing state-level disparities in prime-age male LFPRs by in effect "tying" men to a locality and discouraging their efforts to move in search of opportunity. Here I touch on another possible effect—the role of probation and

parole in "tying" male offenders to a locality and preventing movement in search of work. With over 4 million male offenders today under such correctional supervision—the overwhelming majority of them in the prime working ages—this effect may be nontrivial.

6. "Prevalence of Imprisonment in the U.S. Population," Bureau of Justice Statistics, last modified August 2003, http://www.bjs.gov/content/pub/ascii/piuspo1.txt.

7. What are some of the things we *don't* know about these 20 million Americans? Well, let's begin with family life: we don't how many children they have, their marital status, who they live with, their housing situation. Then there is health: we don't know their mortality rates or life expectancy, their disease and disability profile, their mental health status. Also, employment: we do not know their labor force participation rates, unemployment rates, jobs by sector, or wages. Apart from broad generalities, we know roughly nothing about their education patterns, skills, or training. You can't find any official data on their sources of income, taxes paid, or social services consumed either. We could keep going, but the point by now should be clear: in a polity where information guides public policy, people with a felony conviction in their background appear to be of little concern to the rest of us unless their behavior constitutes a clear and present menace to society.

8. One of the few exceptions is John Schmitt and Kris Warner, "Ex-offenders and the Labor Market," Center for Economic and Policy Research, last modified November 2010, http://cepr.net/documents/publications/ex-offenders-2010-11.pdf.

9. The NLSY collects information on the arrest history and incarceration history of the men and women it follows over time. The NLSY follows two birth cohorts: the first being men and women born between 1957 and 1964, first interviewed in 1979 and now reinterviewed every two years, and a second group of men and women born in the 1980–84 period, who were first interviewed in 1997 and also are reinterviewed every two years. The NLSY survey thus today offers a window on the employment–criminal history relationship for one group of men (the 1957–64 cohort) over almost the entire course of their entire prime-age working life and for another younger group of men (the 1980–84 cohort) who are now just at the beginning of their prime working ages.

10. The other is the Panel Study of Income Dynamics, although its information is more limited. For more information see "The Panel Study of Income Dynamics—PSID—Is the Longest Running Longitudinal Household Survey in the World," PSID, http://psidonline.isr.umich.edu/, and "The Child Development Supplement Transition into Adulthood Study 2009: User Guide," PSID, http://psidonline.isr.umich.edu/CDS/TA09_UserGuide.pdf.

11. Why are criminal-class men more likely to be out of work? How much of this dynamic is due to discrimination by prospective employers? To restrictions on employment occupation or job sector proscribed by law? To low education and skills? To the loss of skills after involvement with the criminal justice system? To off-the-books work, whether licit or illicit? To disinclination to work at legitimate but lower-paying jobs? At the moment, we possess precious little in the way of data-based answers to these questions. But these are questions we urgently need answers to if we are to have much hope of raising work rates for this enormous population.

CHAPTER 10

1. Charles Murray, "The Coming of Custodial Democracy," *Commentary*, September 1, 1988, https://www.commentarymagazine.com/articles/the-coming-of-custodial-democracy/. In that essay, Murray considered the possibility of a dystopic political future "in which a substantial portion of our population . . . will be in effect treated as wards of the state."

2. Ian Hathaway and Robert E. Litan, "Declining Business Dynamism in the United States: A Look at States and Metros," Brookings Institution, last modified May 2014, http://www.brookings.edu/~/media/research/files/papers/2014/05/declining-business-dynamism-litan/declining_business_dynamism_hathaway_litan.pdf.

3. Ibid., 1.

4. Raven Malloy et al., "Understanding Declining Fluidity in the U.S. Labor Market," Brookings Institution, last modified March 10–11, 2016, http://www.brookings.edu/~/media/projects/bpea/spring-2016/molloyetal_decliningfluiditylabormarket_conferencedraft.pdf.

5. Marie-Joseé Kravis, "What's Killing Jobs and Stalling the Economy," *Wall Street Journal*, June 3, 2016, http://www.wsj.com/articles/whats-killing-jobs-and-stalling-the-economy-1464992963.
6. Hanming Fang and Michael P. Keane, "Assessing the Impact of Welfare Reform on Single Mothers," Brookings Institution, last modified 2004, http://www.brookings.edu/about/projects/bpea/papers/2004/welfare-reform-single-mothers-fang.
7. Between 1990 and 2010, the estimated share of nonincarcerated felons in America's adult population nearly doubled—but over that same period, crime rates in America plunged. According to the Bureau of Justice Statistics National Crime Victimization Survey, between 1993 and 2014 (the full range of the data series now available), America's rate of victimization for property crime dropped by nearly two-thirds and the rate for violent crime dropped by nearly three-fourths (cf. Jennifer L. Truman and Lynn Langton, "Criminal Victimization, 2014," figure 1, Bureau of Justice Statistics, http://www.bjs.gov/content/pub/pdf/cv14.pdf, "NCVS Victimization Analysis Tool (NVAT)," Bureau of Justice Statistics, http://www.bjs.gov/index.cfm?ty=nvat). To be sure, there is still plenty of room for improvement with regard to crime prevention in America. Suffice it here to observe that, at least to date, the extraordinary increase in the number of sentenced felons among us has not prevented dramatic overall advances in public safety.

CHAPTER 11

1. See Historical Federal Workforce Tables, U.S. Office of Personnel Management, https://www.opm.gov/policy-data-oversight/data-analysis-documentation/federal-employment-reports/historical-tables/total-government-employment-since-1962/.

CHAPTER 12

1. Louis Uchitelle and David Leonhardt, *New York Times*, "Men Not Working, and Not Wanting Just Any Job," July 31, 2006, http://www.nytimes.com/2006/07/31/business/31men.html?_r=1.
2. Isaac Shapiro et. al., Center on Budget and Policy Priorities, "It Pays

to Work: Work Incentives and the Safety Net," March 3, 2016, http://www.cbpp.org/research/federal-tax/it-pays-to-work-work-incentives-and-the-safety-net..

CHAPTER 13

1. Hanming Fang and Michael P. Keane, "Assessing the Impact of Welfare Reform on Single Mothers," *Brookings Papers on Economic Activity* 1 (2004): 1–116. https://www.brookings.edu/wp-content/uploads/2004/01/2004a_bpea_fang.pdf.

About the Contributors

JARED BERNSTEIN joined the Center on Budget and Policy Priorities in May 2011 as a Senior Fellow. From 2009 to 2011, Bernstein was the chief economist and economic advisor to Vice President Joe Biden, executive director of the White House Task Force on the Middle Class, and a member of President Obama's economic team.

NICHOLAS EBERSTADT, a political economist by training, holds the Henry Wendt Chair in Political Economy at the American Enterprise Institute and is a senior advisor to the National Bureau of Asian Research. He researches and writes extensively on demographics, economic development, and international security. His many books and monographs include *A Nation of Takers: America's Entitlement Epidemic* (Templeton Press, 2012). Eberstadt earned his AB, MPA, and PhD at Harvard and his MSc at the London School of Economics. In 2012, he was awarded the Bradley Prize.

HENRY OLSEN, currently a Senior Fellow at the Ethics and Public Policy Center, has worked in senior executive positions at many center-right think tanks. He most recently served from 2006 to 2013 as vice president and director of the National Research Initiative at the American Enterprise Institute. He previously worked as vice president of programs at the Manhattan Institute and president of the Commonwealth Foundation. Mr. Olsen's work has been featured in many prominent publications, including the *Wall Street Journal,* the *Washington Post, National Review,* and the *Weekly Standard.* He is the author of the forthcoming book, *Ronald Reagan: New Deal Conservative* (HarperCollins, 2017).